Early Pennsylvania Hardware

Written and Illustrated
by
Herbert Schiffer

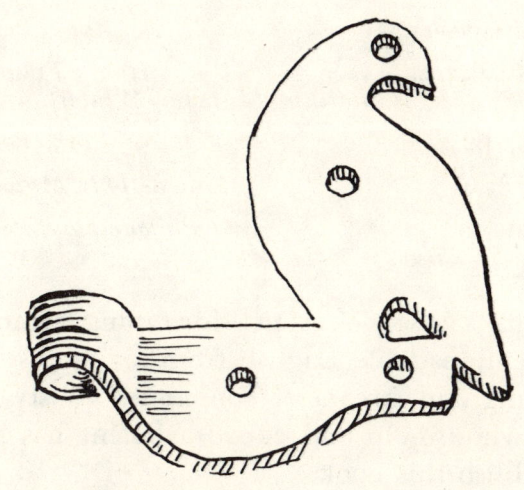

Schiffer Publishing Ltd

Box E, Exton, Pennsylvania 19341

Acknowledgments

My most heartfelt thanks to the following people who, have taken time from their busy lives to either answer innumerable questions, or generously allowed me to sketch and photograph many of the fine examples of hardware.

BART ANDERSON	Chester County Historical Society, West Chester, Pennsylvania
WHITMAN BALL	Exton, Pennsylvania
MONROE COLDRON	West Chester, Pennsylvania
ERIC DEJONGE	William Penn Memorial Museum Harrisburg, Pennsylvania
TITUS C. GEESEY	Wilmington, Delaware
WALTER HIMMELREICH	Ronk, Pennsylvania
CHARLES HUMMELL	Henry Francis duPont Winterthur Museum, Winterthur, Delaware
JOE KINDIG, JR.	York, Pennsylvania
HENRI MARCEAU	Philadelphia Museum of Art
ROBERT TRUMP	Philadelphia, Pennsylvania

and to MRS. YVONNE Y. ALLEN for typing, arranging and making semi-readable English from my fantastically bad handwriting and stream of conscious. . . .style, and to my wife whose help and encouragement has prompted me to publish this book.

About the Author

Herbert Schiffer was born in New York City in 1917 and attended the Lawrenceville and Avon Schools and Cornell University.

While farming near West Chester, Pennsylvania, the author joined the staff of the Henry F. duPont Winterthur Museum.

Since 1954 he has been in the Art and Antique business at Exton, Pennsylvania and is a member of the Art and Antique Dealers Society of America.

Contents

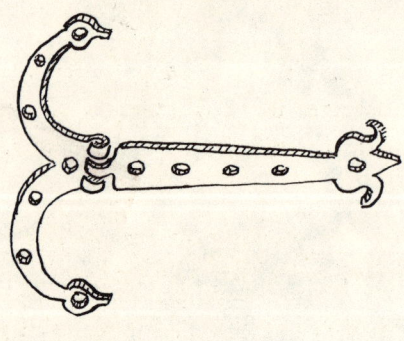

Introduction 1
Thumb Latches 3
Brass Box Locks 8
Mortise Locks 10
Keyhole Plate Latches 13
Fakes 14
Square Plate Latches 16
Iron Box Locks 18
Carpenter Locks 20
Victorian Cast Iron Locks 24
Dutch Elbow Locks 26
Moravian Locks 31
Wooden Locks 32
Knobs 35
Rosettes 37
Knobs and Stirrups 38
Hinges 40
Strap Hinges 43
Pintles 45
Hasps 46
Keys 48
Keyhole Escutcheons 50
Shutter Fasteners 53
Footscrapers 54
Brass Knockers 56
Iron Knockers 58
How to Learn More
About Pennsylvania Hardware 60
And Annotated Bibliography 61
Key to Art 63

Introduction

The sole purpose of this book is to be helpful and to answer the most frequent questions of architects, restorers or just laymen who are trying to correctly restore a period room.

The problem in writing this book has not been what to say and what to show — but rather the contrary.

To thoroughly cover one subject, such as hardware on shutters would take an entire book this size. The question occurs would anyone be interested in such a book?

I think that it is a great shame that so many restorations have turned to reproduction hardware at enormous expense, when, for about the same cost and a little more effort, sufficient and correct period hardware can be obtained.

There is little reason why anyone armed with the information in this book, some money, but more patience, cannot buy the appropriate period hardware for one room, or, for that matter, the entire house and its outbuildings. People who have invested small fortunes in their homes and furnishings often feel reluctant to tackle what seems to be the monumental task of selecting the right hardware.

This book, I hope, will give them the needed encouragement to pursue the task of finding the correct period hardware and to enjoy the gratifying results that it can give.

There are a few rules to remember when buying period locks to save the sanity of both the purchaser and the dealer.

You Must know

1. Thickness of the door
2. Hinges, left or right
3. Height available for lock (rail size)
4. Desirable limits of size of lock

A Right Hand door is shown above

2

Thumb Latches

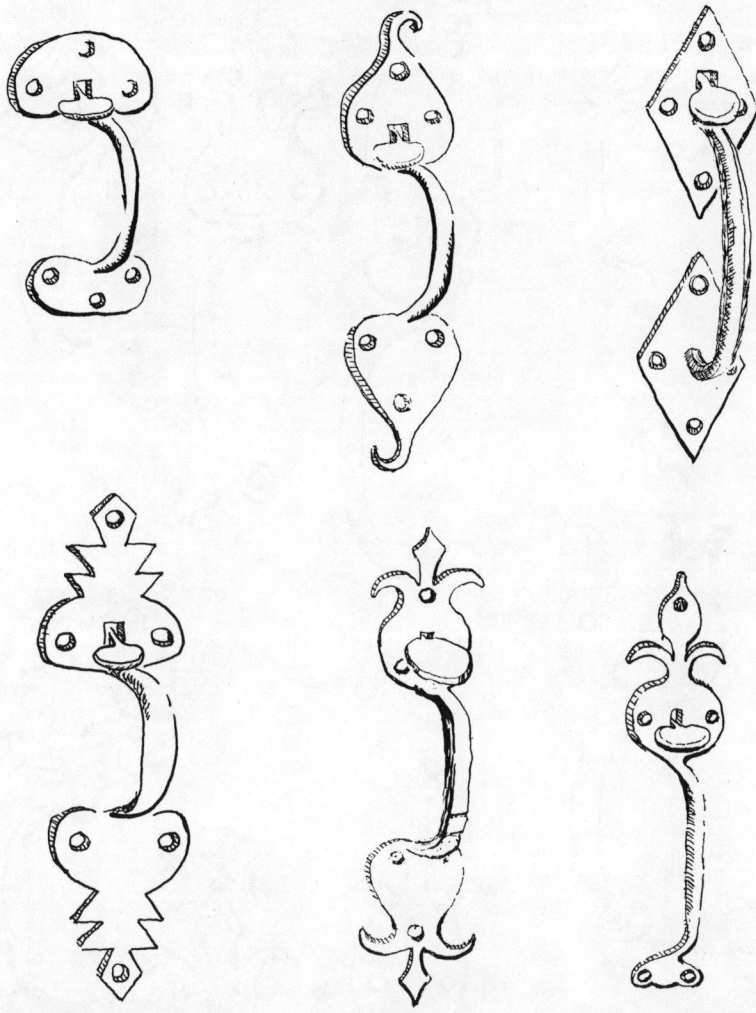

Thumb Latches as illustrated above are inexpensive, readily available and can be correctly used on Pennsylvania houses.

On this page are shown examples of the types most frequently found in Pennsylvania.

Bean	Tulip Bud	Diamond
Pine Tree	Tulip	Tulip

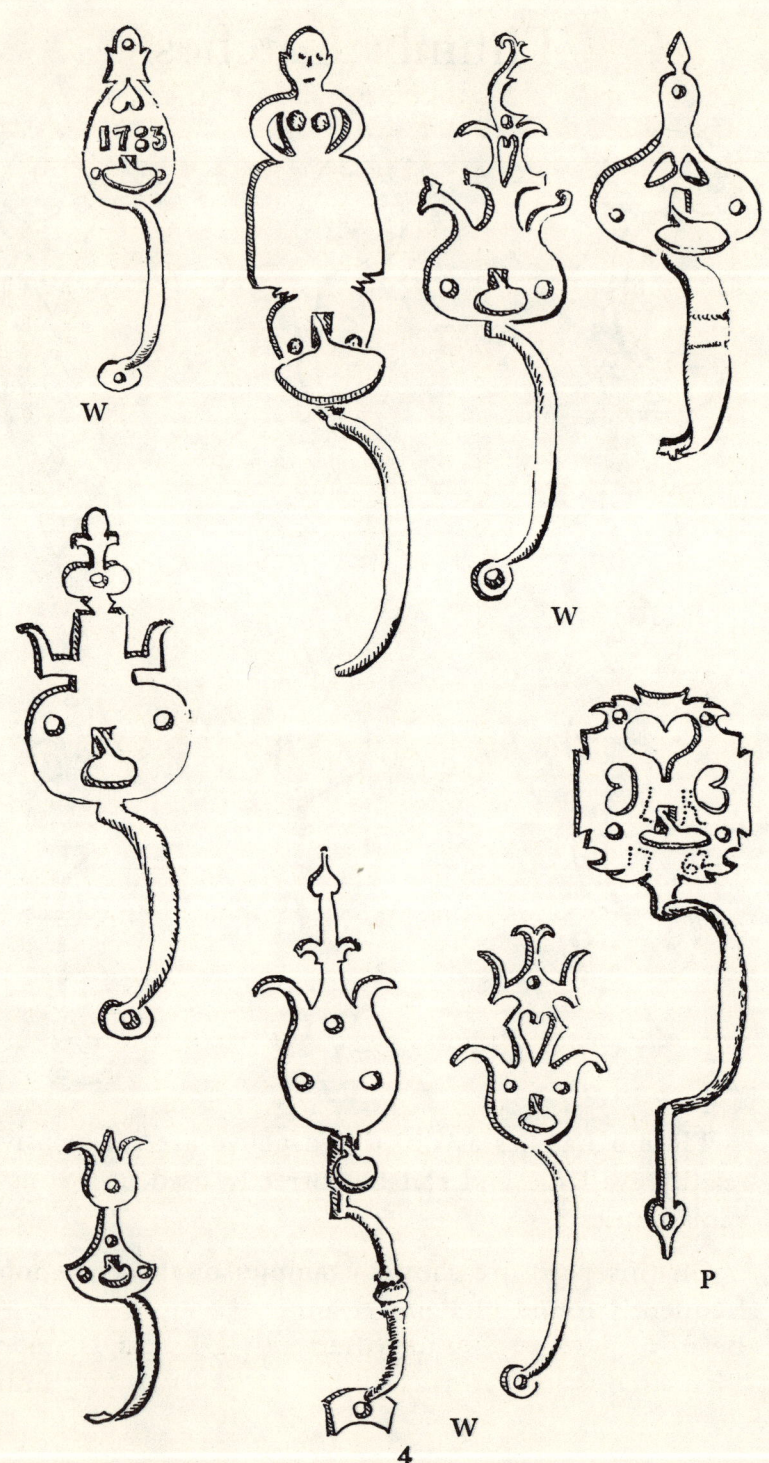

W

W

W

P

4

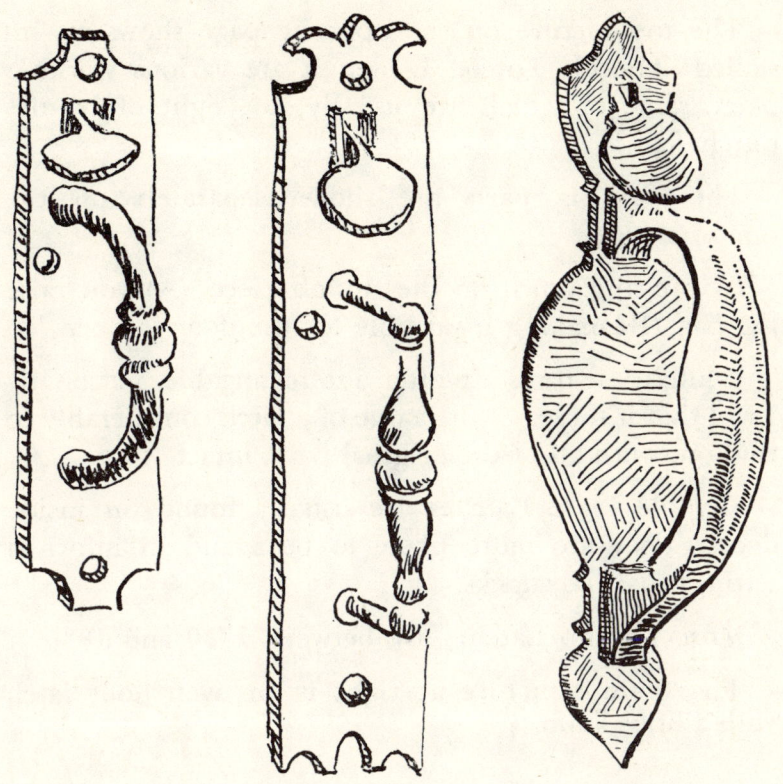

All of the Thumb Latches shown on Page 4 are of superior (museum) quality and are almost impossible to find.

The Period of Hand Forged Hardware ended about 1860. The artistically designed early latches were followed by the period of mass-produced latches, of which many were supplied with cast iron handles. The two illustrations on the left of this page, are typical of the decline of stylistic imagination and individual craftsmanship. The latch on the right is brass, a type mostly found in New England, although occasionally found in Pennsylvania. This type of brass latch was generally made between 1780 and 1820. Most of them were made in England.

The top picture on the opposite page shows an installed Thumb Latch. Under it are various working parts, same of which are usually lost sight of by the purchaser.

The working parts are shown separately on the opposite page.

'By pressing down on the thumb piece (A) you raise the bar (B) making it possible for the door to open.

While these parts are often interchangable, personally I feel that it increases the value of a latch considerably to find one with all of the original parts intact.

Keyhole Plate Latches are usually found on inside doors. They are more likely to be found in informal settings than box locks.

Most Thumb Latches are between 1730 and 1830.

The bottom picture at right is an oven door latch with a brass knob.

Interior Locking Device of a Thumb Latch

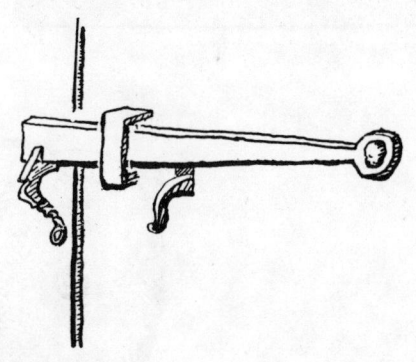

A   *Thumb Latch*

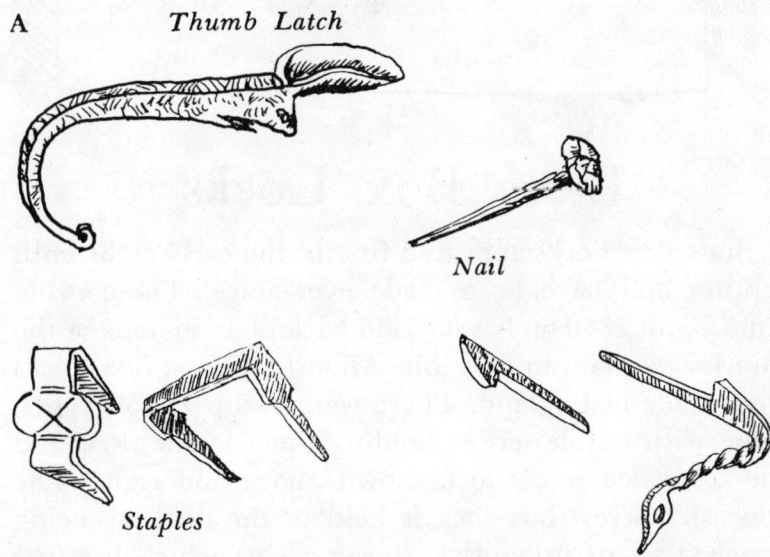

Nail

Staples   *Keepers*

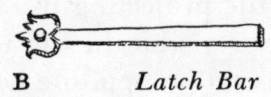

B   *Latch Bar*

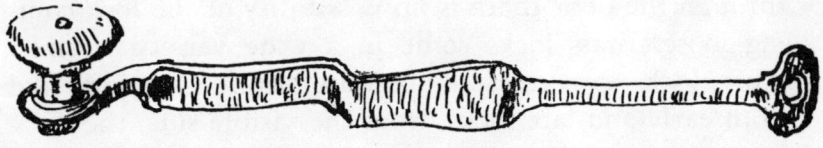

7

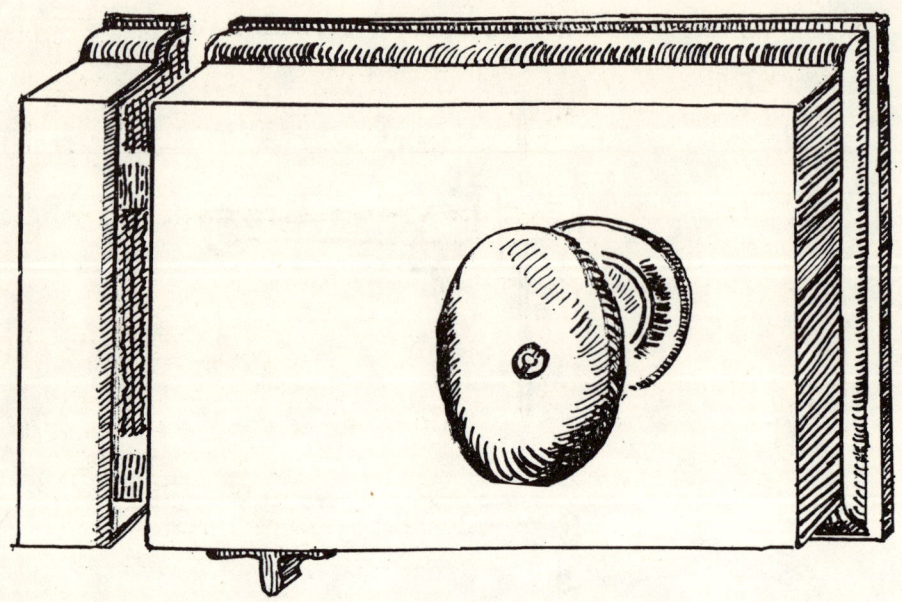

Brass Box Locks

Brass Box Locks appeared first in the early eighteenth century and have been made ever since. Those made from about 1830 on have a solid back plate so none of the interior mechanism is visible. Almost all Brass Box Locks were made in England. There were two principle types, those with visible screws holding them to the door and the concealed screw lock shown above and right. The concealed screw box lock is held to the door by being attached to an iron plate (lower right) which has first been screwed to the door. The brass concealed screw lock is then slid behind the projecting iron arms on the iron back plate. One screw visible in the middle of the left hand side of the illustration opposite holds the brass lock securely to the iron plate. Once the knob shaft is pushed through the door there is no possibility of the lock coming loose. Brass locks come in a wide variety of sizes. This lock was selected because while looking like both early and late locks, from the visible side, the back shows many of the refinements found only on early locks

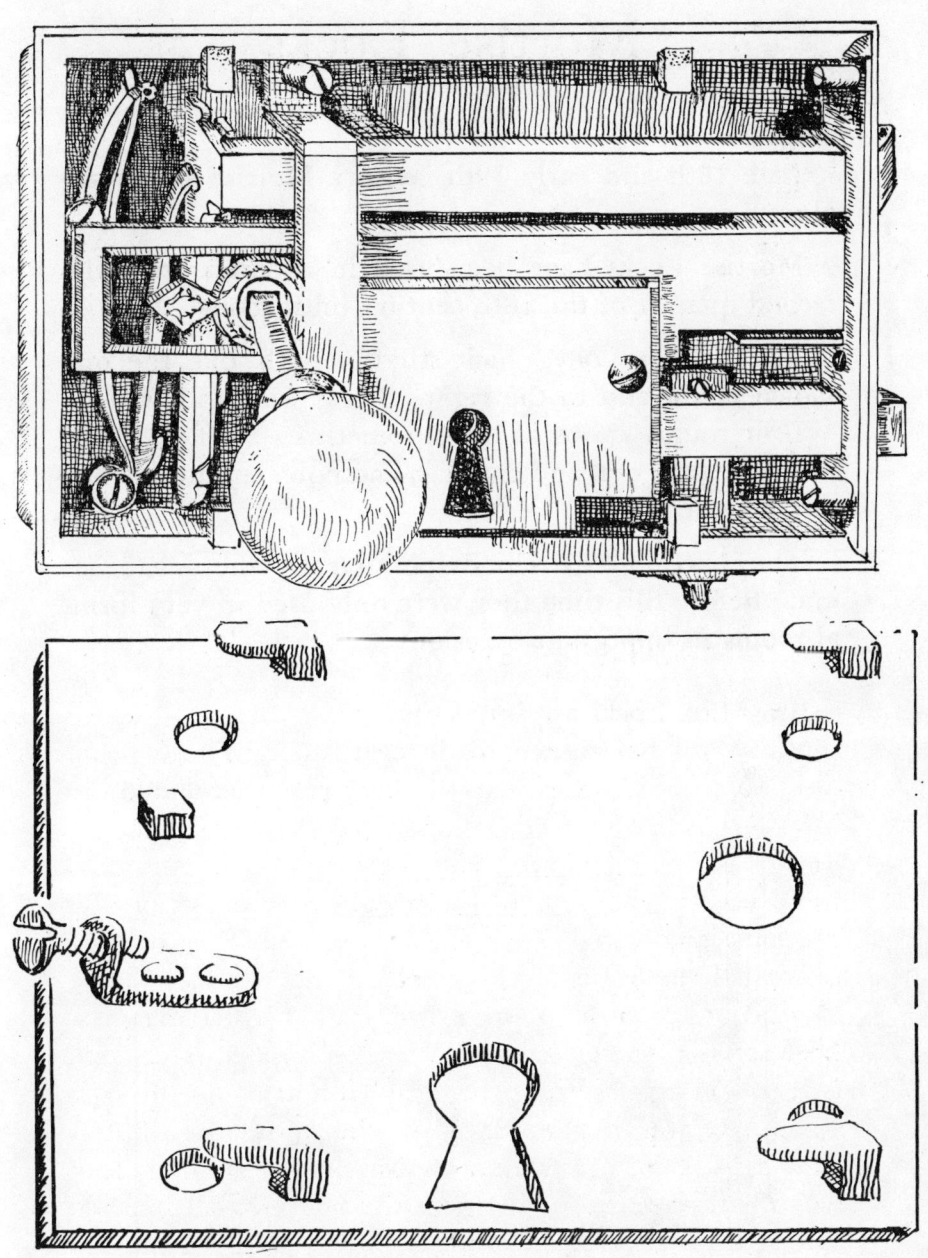

such as chamfering, engraving, a small lock plate, and the coarse irregularity of the screw thread. Both visible and concealed screw brass locks were made with plain or moulded edges (note upper left) during the same period.

9

Mortise Locks

Late 18th and early 19th century Mortise Locks are almost non-existent today.

Mortise Locks have been used in America from the second quarter of the 18th century until today.

The earliest ones had stirrup pulls like the one shown below and to the right. These were followed by oval or round knobs of brass, sometimes Sheffield silver in the Federal era, and cut glass and porcelain in the Victorian period.

They became extremely popular in the Victorian era. Before this time they were only used in very formal rooms in important mansions.

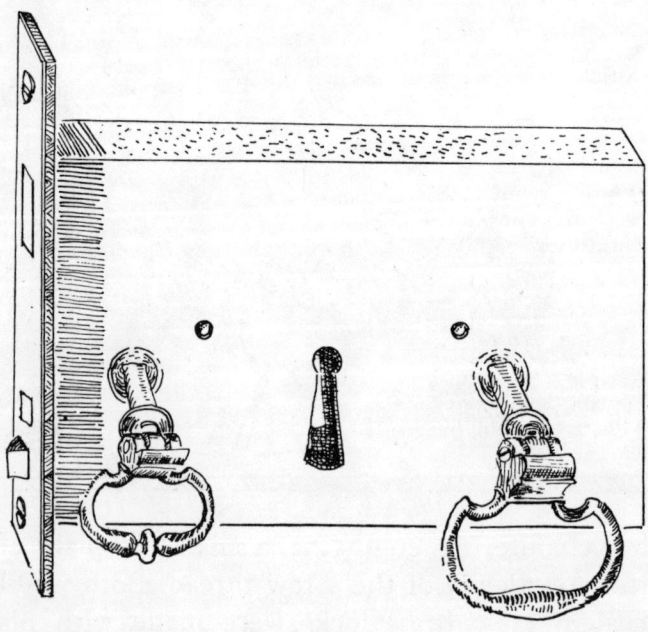

10

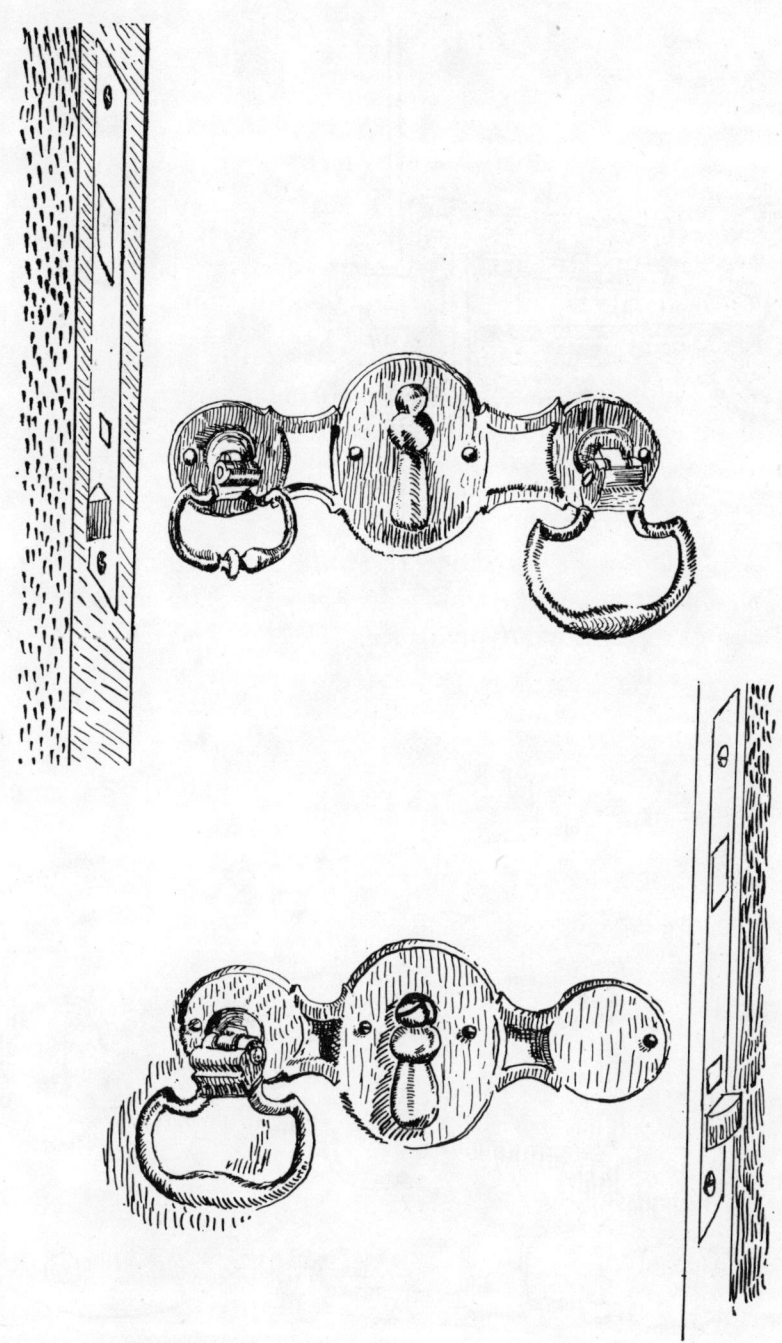

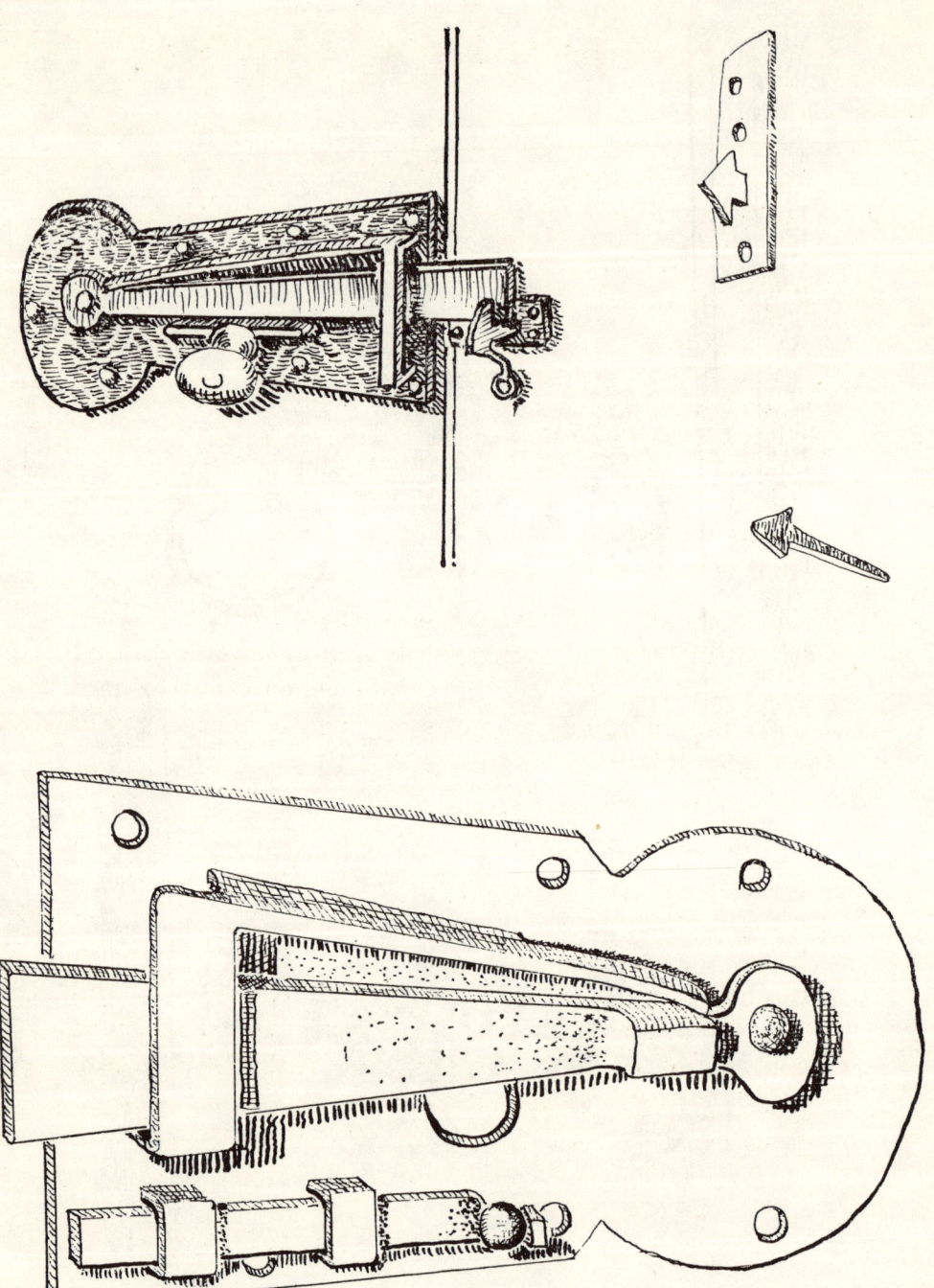

Keyhole Plate Latches

Keyhole Plate Latches generally date from the end of the 17th century to about 1820, and vary from three to thirteen inches in lenght, but average five inches.

Early iron hardware was generally painted the color of the door itself. It is a fairly modern tradition to show the hardware in a black paint or steel brushed and oiled. Most of the latches taken out of old houses have many layers of paint of the colors in which the rooms were painted.

Keyhole Latches were rarely on front doors, but were mostly found on interior doors, closets and doors to stairs.

Almost all these latches are of English origin. I have seen many marked examples. Bills and ledgers existing for some of the most important American mansions show the enormous amounts of English hardware that was imported.

Upper left is shown the Keyhole Latch complete with a fairly unusual keeper. The more usual types of keepers are shown at the right of the drawing. The keeper in the top illustration is the one we recommend. Shown lower left is an early type of Keyhole Plate Latch without its cam, shaft, or knobs, but with an early type of night bolt. The spring on this type works contrary to what would be considered sensible leverage, but still it works well after 150 years. The night latch knob is solid wrought iron.

13

The Upper right keyhole plate with a later type of spring, is shown without its cam, shaft and knobs.

Lower right is shown the earlier type of spring with the cam in place but without the shaft and knobs.

These are beautifully simple. You turn the knob, the square shaft makes the cam lift the latch bar against the gentle pressure of the spring. The spring holds the latch down unless the knob is turned.

Both keyhole plate latches and square plate latches come with either round or oval knobs. Some of the earliest come with stirrup handles. Some of the night bolts have iron knobs, some are brass with an iron shaft riveted through (see square plate latch upper right page 17). This is a nice refinement and earlier than the type of night latch seen in the picture of square plate latches lower right.

Fakes

There are many fake hinges, latches, locks and other hardware.

Some fakes are very good. I have been fooled and so will you. Just try to keep a good average. Your average should improve after years of making mistakes. I hope mine has.

Things that would make one look more suspiciously at a piece of iron would be:

Sharp edges   Little play or wear in hinges
Very even rusting   Evenly spaced hammer indentation
Thicker metal than known old examples.

The best answer to this problem is to buy from reputable and knowledgable dealers.

14

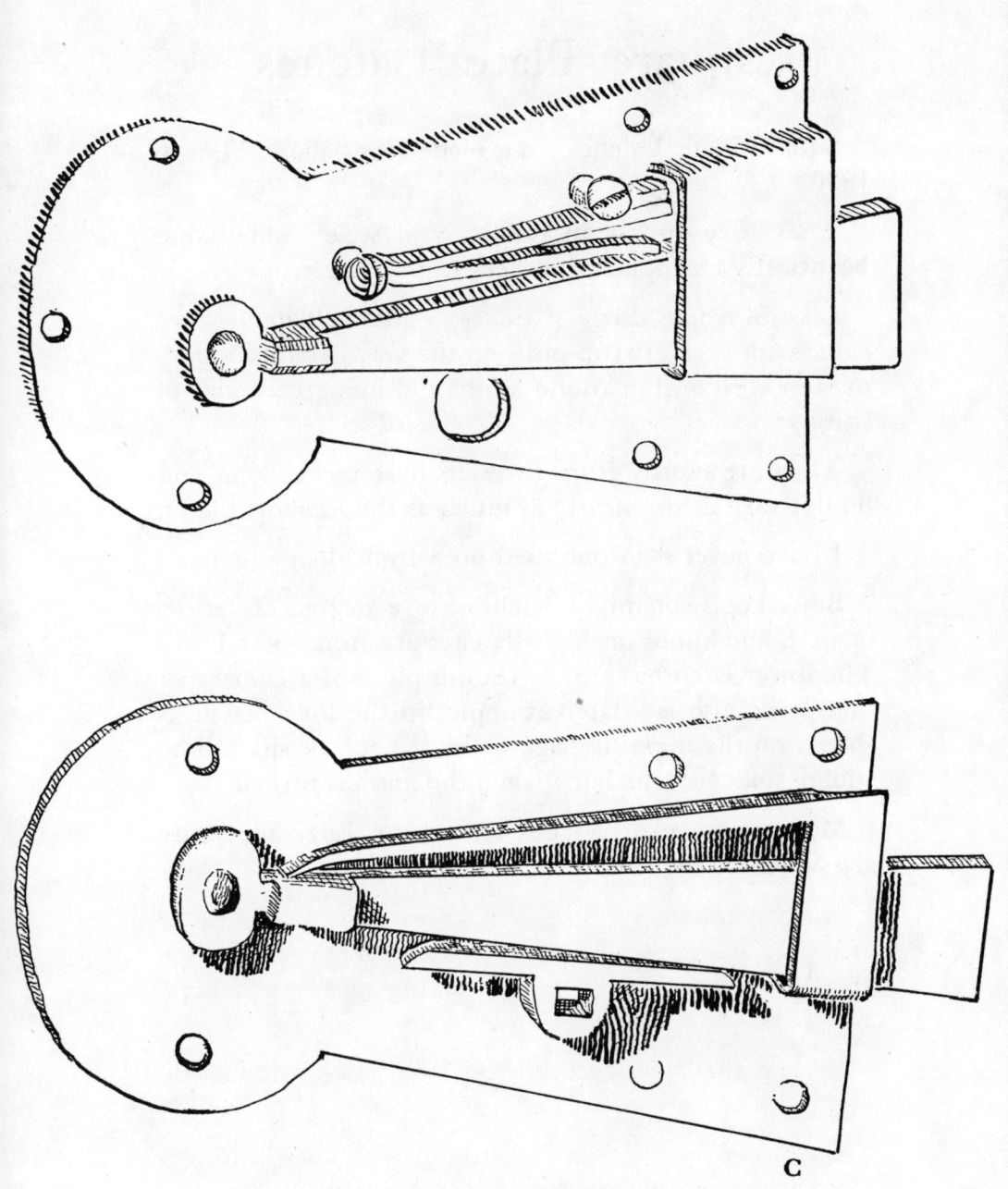

C

Square Plate Latches

1730 –
1830 .

Square Plate Latches were made from about 1730 to 1830.

They vary greatly in quality and style. Some were beautifully champhered, others were quite crude.

Like Keyhole Plate Latches, Square Plate Latches come with brass stirrup pulls on the very early examples, or later with oval or round knobs and in a great range of sizes.

They are mostly from three to four inches long and do not vary in size nearly as much as the Keyhole plates.

I have never seen one used on a front door.

Brass knobs on night latches are a degree of refinement. Some knobs on night latches are iron, some brass. The lower latch has a brass thumb piece of a later type, the spring also is a later example, in the lower latch as shown on the oppoiste page without knob or shaft. The square shaft lifts the latch when the knob is turned.

Most square plate latches came from England. Many are signed by their makers.

16

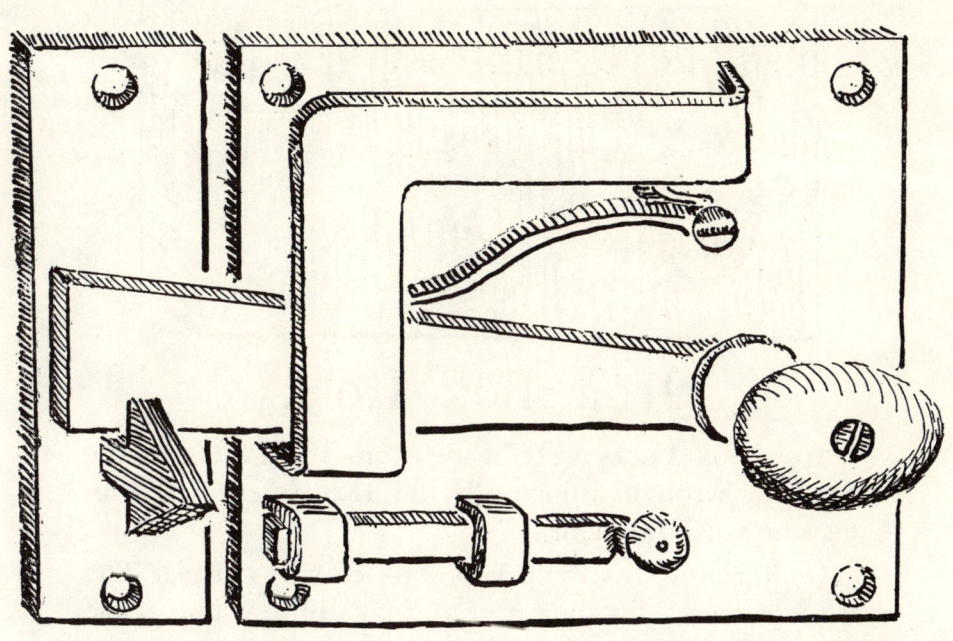

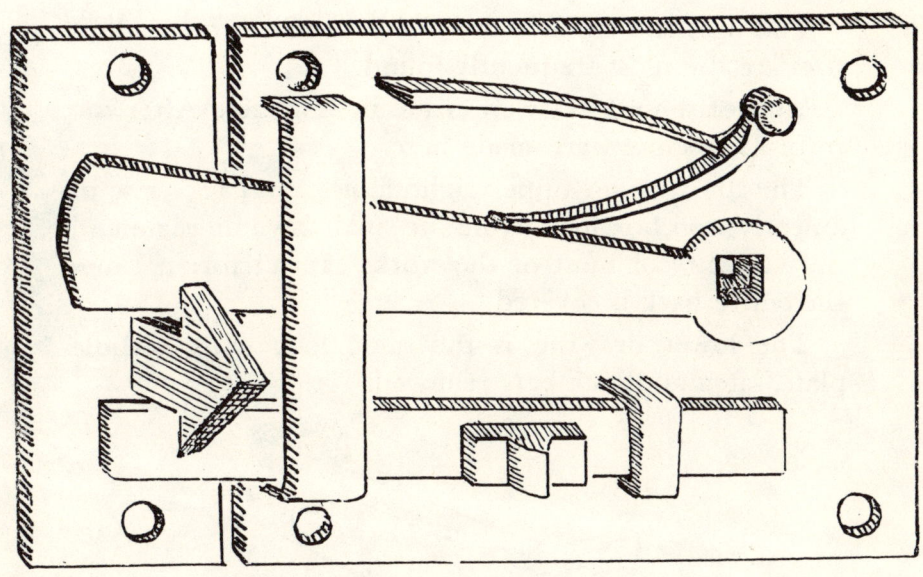

17

Iron Box Locks

1720 -
1820

Iron Box Locks were made from the 1720's to the 1820's of wrought iron until after 1820 when caste iron became more frequent.

Oval, round or stirrup knobs are equally correct. The stirrups are by far the rarest and possibly earliest. Some keepers had a brass rim (see bottom of page).

This type of lock is found very frequently in Pennsylvania. Some entire houses have this type of lock in both formal and informal rooms.

The sizes run from 3" x 4" to 9" x 12". The smallest sizes are the most frequently found.

Most of these locks were made in England. After the revolution some were made here.

The drawing on upper right shows the back view of an early iron box lock. Note the small keyhole plate and the visibility of most of the works. In Victorian times the entire back is covered.

The lower drawing is the same lock with keyhole plate, latch and lock bars removed.

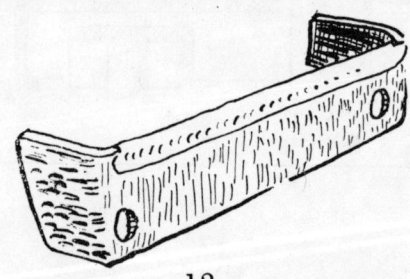

18

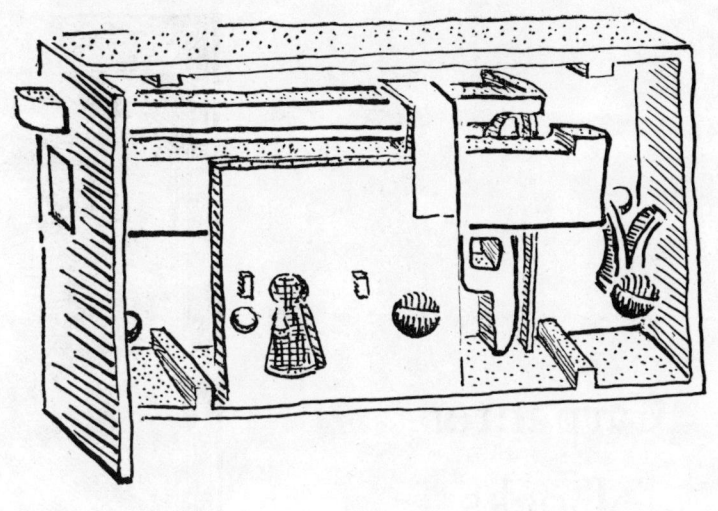

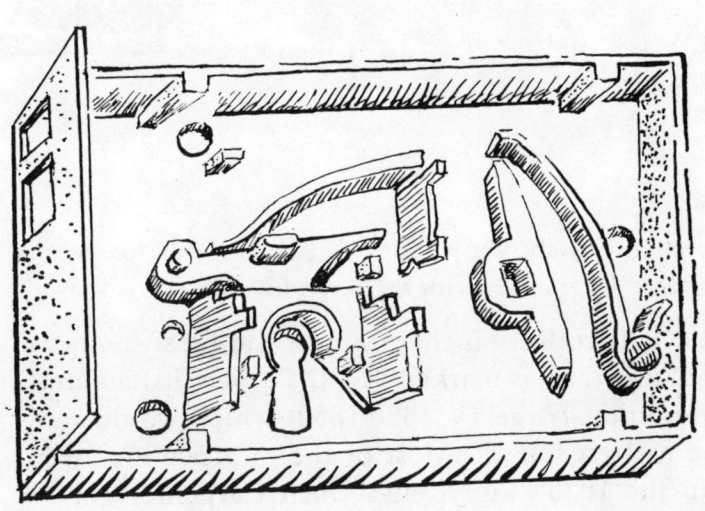

Carpenter Locks

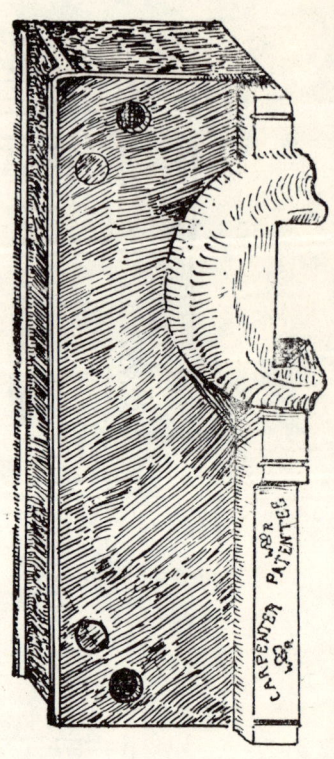

The example shown with "W.R." on the keeper is the earliest "Carpenter" lock I have found.

In the Ball collection there is just the brass mounted keeper of one that is marked "G.R. Carpenter Patantee" (We presume George IV 1820-1830) which would indicate the earliest found. Most of the "Carpenters" were made in the 1830's and 1840's when Carpenter got his patent.

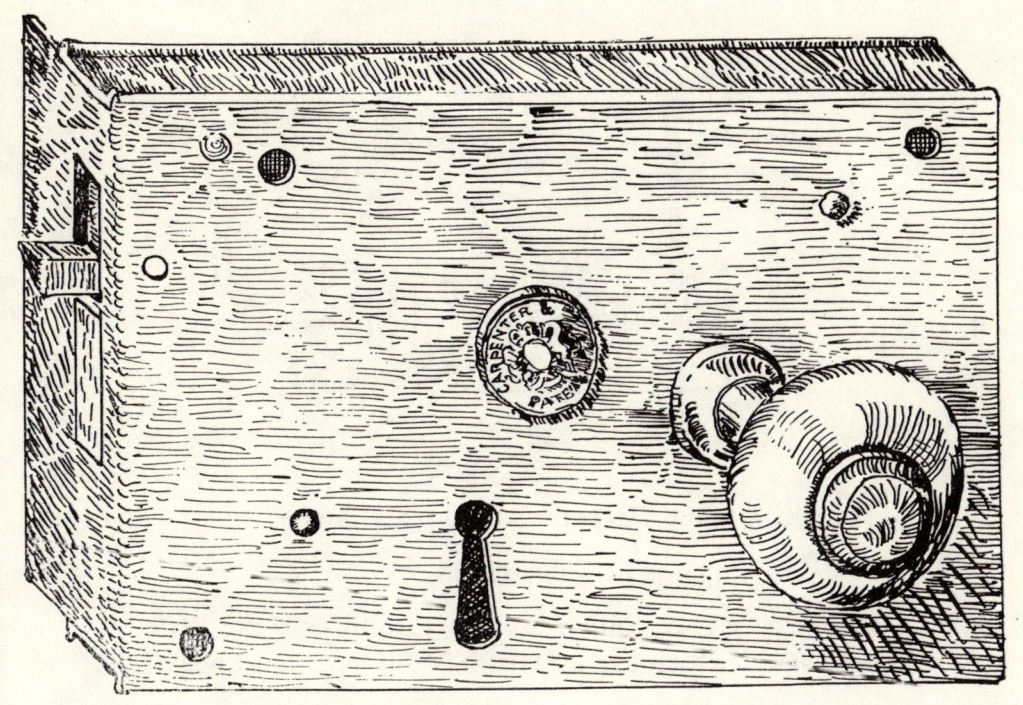

The factor that makes them different is that turning the knob raises the bar latch. In earlier types the bar moves in a horizontal manner.

Many of the "Carpenters" were made by other firms. but an iron lock with a raising bar and a small brass plaque and a brass bound keeper is called a Carpenter type.

The first eight "Carpenter" locks I picked off our shelves were made by eight different makers.

21

There are many Carpenter type plate latches.

The one shown is by John Povey.

Shown at right, double sized are four of these little brass plagues which are a feature of "Carpenter Locks."

Carpenter Locks" were very popular in the late 1830's and through the 1840's, and were found on doors in our shop where the door dated almost 100 years prior to the invention of the lock.

These locks were often used for replacement hardware. Most of the ones found on doors in my shop say *"Walker and V.R."* (Victoria Regina) on the keeper.

Some of the names found on carpenter locks are

James Tildesley   Carpenter & Tildesley
W. Badger & Co.,   S. Smith
Young's Patent   Carpenter Patents

Many like the three brass locks shown at right merely say "Improved Lock #60" or something else equally non-committal.

Carpenter Locks have a solid back plate like other Victorian locks.

Victorian Cast Iron Locks

After the "Carpenter" came the heavy cast Victorian Locks, one of the most attractive of which is this one on the right with the raised eagle.

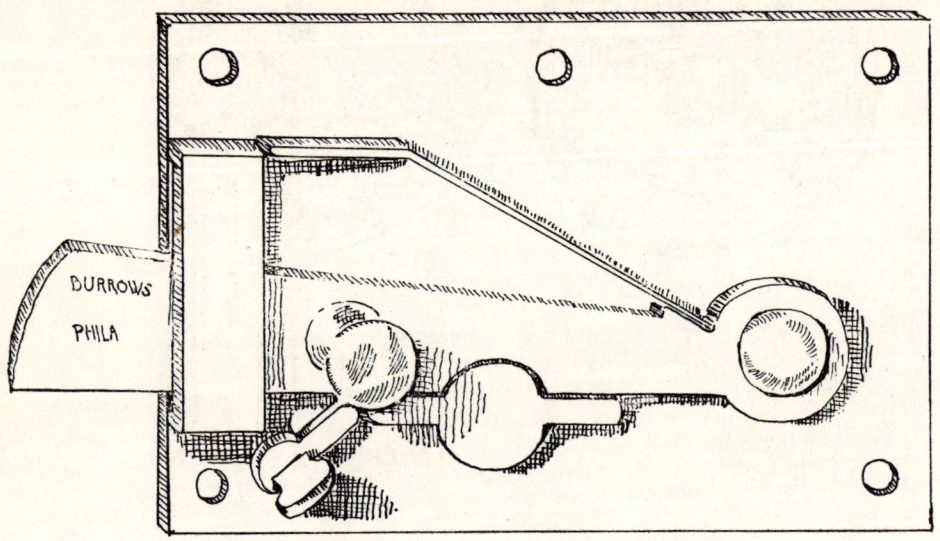

A rare marked Philadelphia Latch, wrought iron, brass, and bell metal.

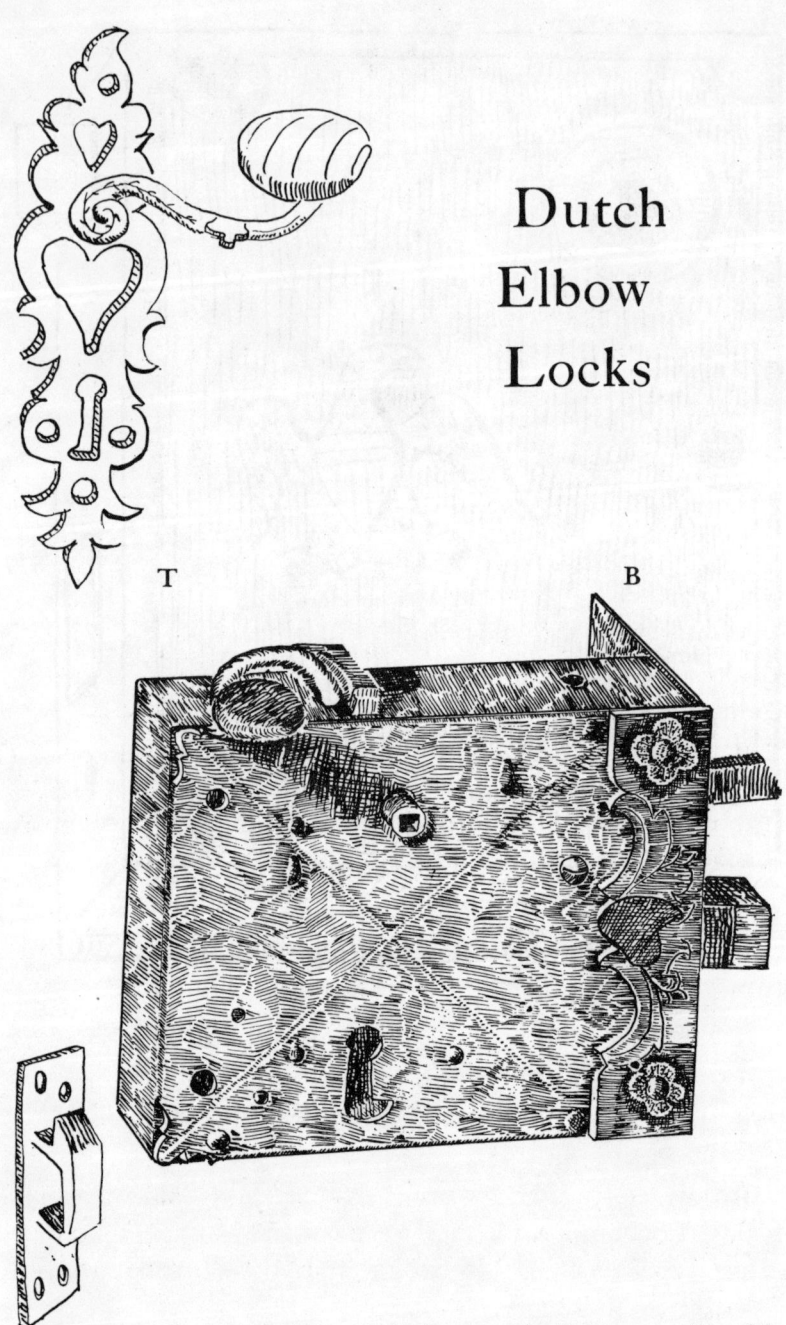

Dutch Elbow Locks

T   B

The small drawings at left is a typical keeper for this type of lock.

26

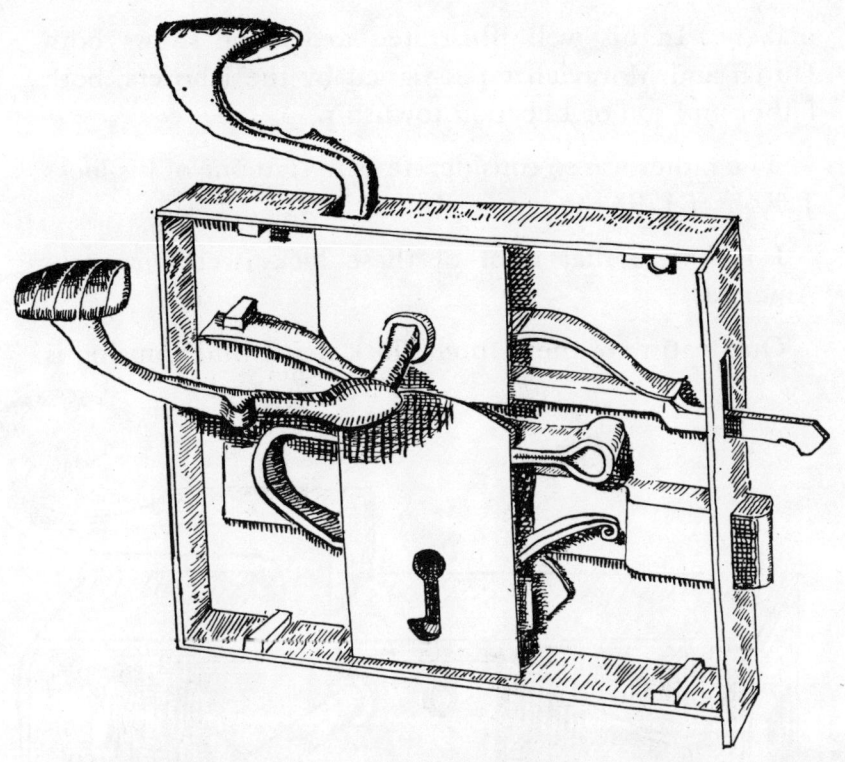

In hundreds of untouched old houses I have seen Dutch Elbow Locks. They were made from the 18th through the 19th century. On this and the facing page we show two early examples.

The top drawing, opposite, shows a very elaborate iron escutenion found on a door with a fine 18th century Dutch Elbow Lock.

They were made more elaborate with a great deal of notching and lines for decoration, both on the side you see and on the works.

Restorations, and restorers seldom use Dutch Elbow Lock and yet I have found more of these than any other type of lock in the English influenced and the Pennsylvania German houses.

Some were undoubtedly made in Germany, but Professor Henry Kaufman's scholarly acticle in "Spinning Wheel" writes about his discovery of the "Rohrer" lock

27

makers. In his well illustrated article he shows both Dutch and Moravian types signed by the Rhorers, both father and son of Lebanon township.

The father was so considerate as to sign one of his locks J. Rohrer 1793 the son D. Rohrer 1822.

I feel sure that most of these locks were made in America.

One feature of the "Dutch" lock that I find amusing is

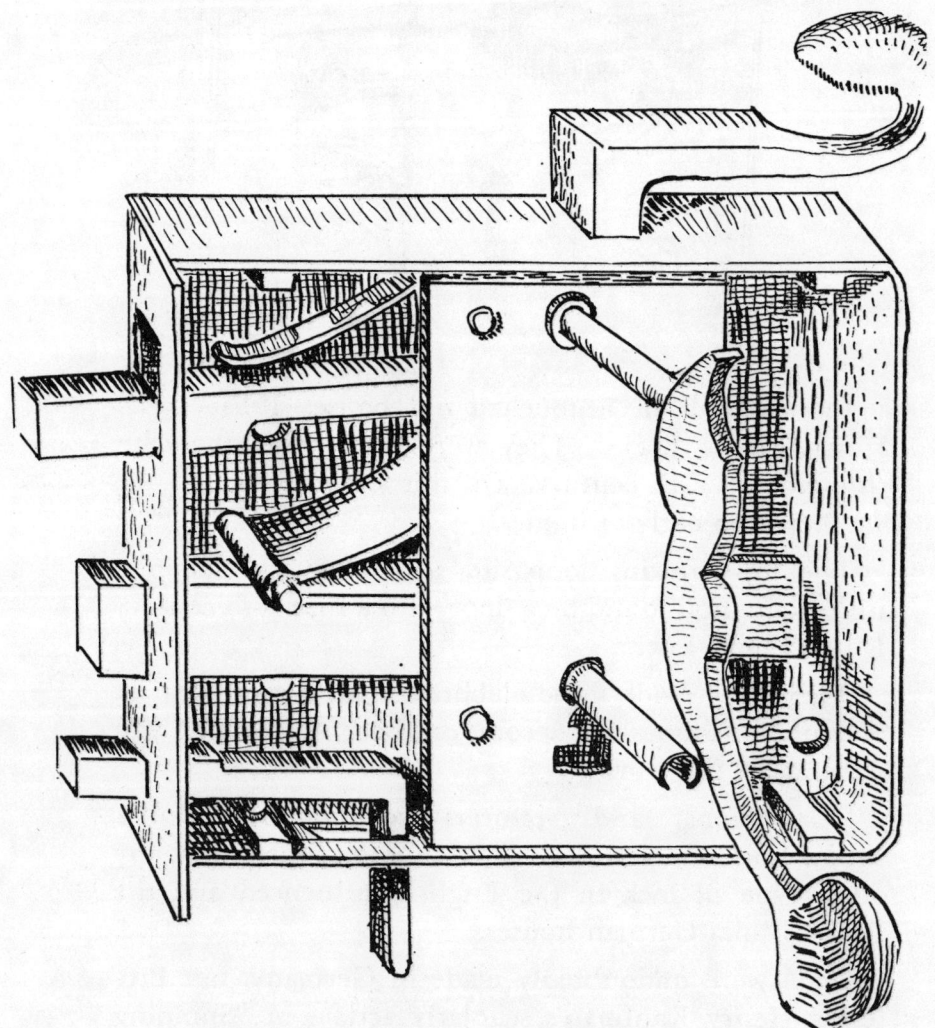

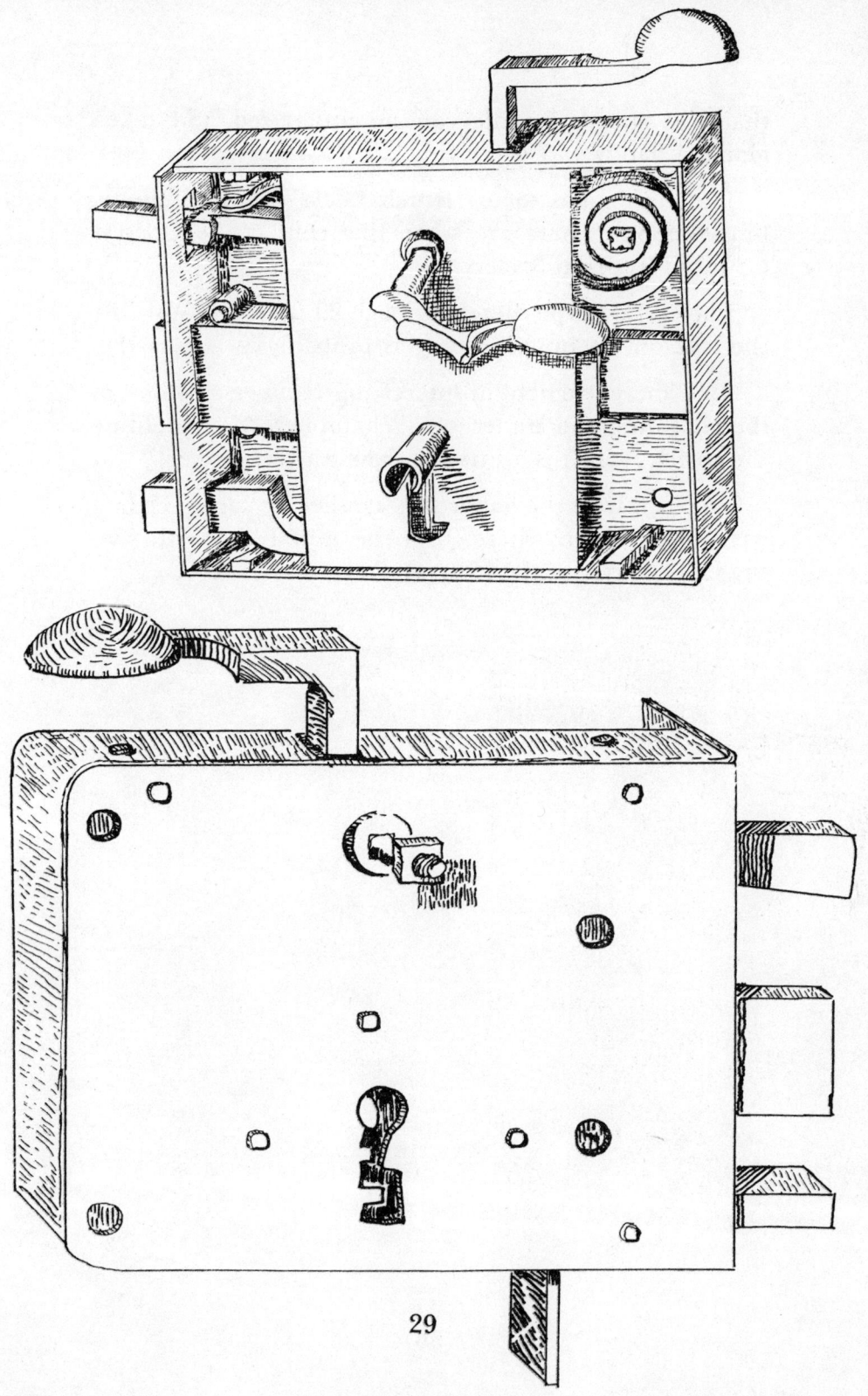

29

that the outside handle can be unscrewed and taken along, a handy way of locking the door.

The author has some "Dutch Locks" with handsome brass knobs. There are some like this at the Chester County Historical Society.

The earliest type shown on page 29 can be 1740 while the lock on the opposite page is probably as late as 180.

Note the extremely uninteresting handles and one of the charming and unnecessary champhered nut holding the spring, which is a survival from an earlier day.

The lock with the handsome handles on the preceding page could be anywhere from the mid 18th century to the first quarter of the 19th century.

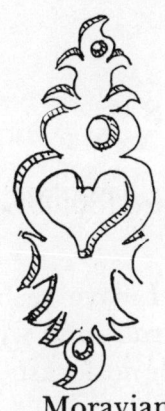

Moravian Locks

T

Moravian Locks are seldom used on restorations.
They should be. I have found hundreds on original doors.

The author recently bought two similar locks that came from Harmony, a communal development in Western Pennsylvania, of the first quarter of the 19th century.

Kaufman's discovery of a signed Rhorer "Moravian" proves they were made here. The full data of this discovery can be found in the August 1965 issue of Spinning Wheel.

I know of no way to tell a lock made in Switzerland or Germany from a lock made by the same man after arriving here - except that many of the foreign locks are often more ornate and decorated.

Mr. Charles Hummel of Winterthur Museum says there was comparatively little commerce between Germany and Pennsylvania so that very few locks could have been imported.

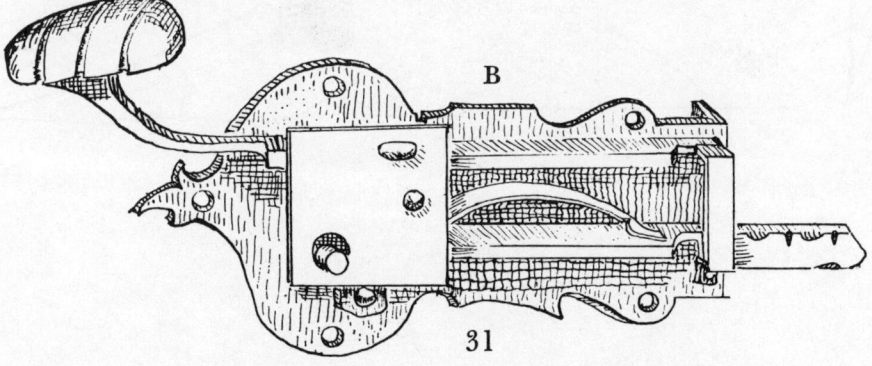

31

Wooden Locks

Wooden Locks or actually lock covers are found both abroad and in America.

Some were made in this country, as I have seen a striped maple case. These locks are quite crude and within the competance of many craftsmen with no locksmith training.

We feel that these should only be used in service rooms, e.g. cellar, pantry and spring house or cabins.

There are some European locks with rather fancy brass bindings. These I have never seen originally used in America.

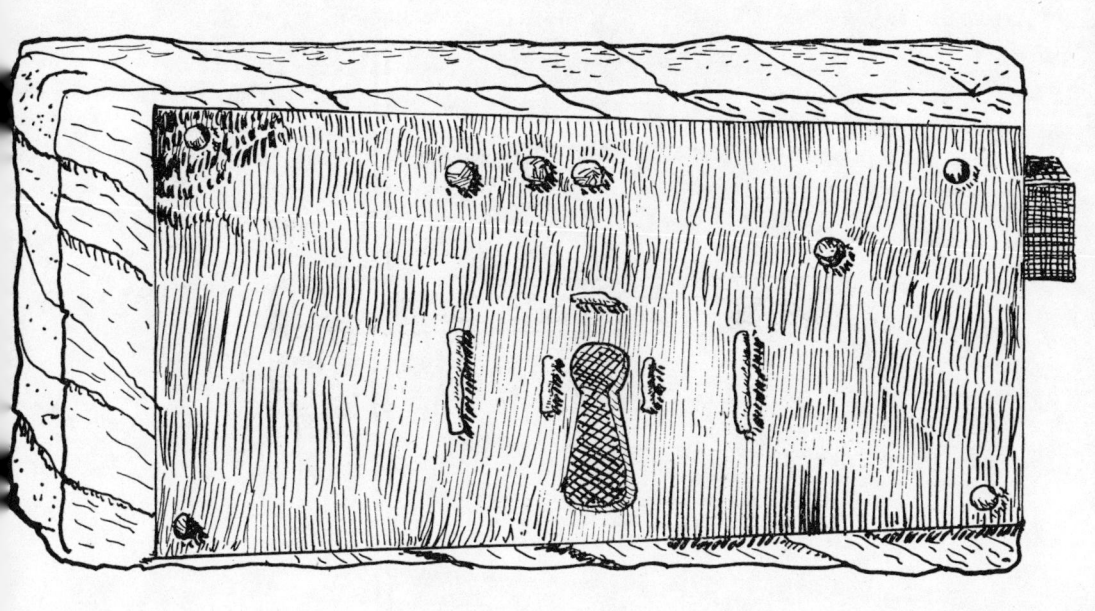

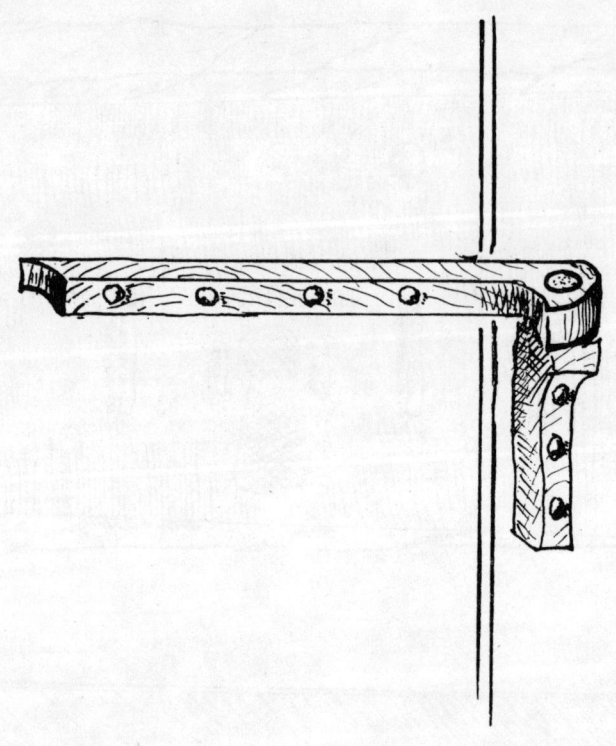

Wooden hinges and latches were frequently used. I have heard of five houses near West Chester which still have them in place. The Historical Architectural Building Survey has pictures available of some in Chester County, Pennsylvania.

Knobs

Round and oval knobs were made during the early 18th century. The knobs on page 36 are shown actual size. Later knobs have heavier and shorter necks.

The earliest round knobs are quite round. By 1780 they are much flatter in cross section. Early knobs are harder to find than early locks. They were usually cast in three parts and silver soldered together.

During the Victorian period, porcelain knobs, both white and brown and pressed glass were used frequently and is what is to be expected on a lock such as the cast iron lock with the eagle or late mortice locks.

35

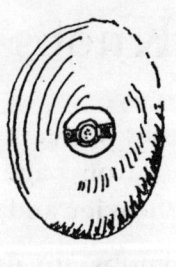

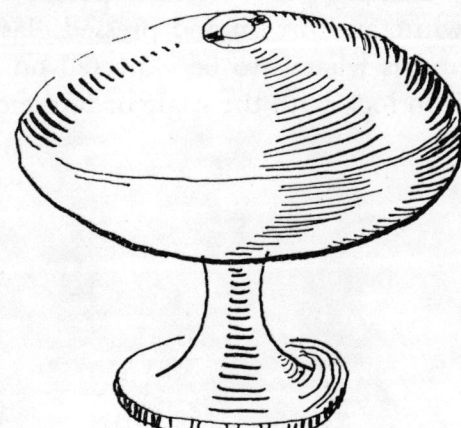

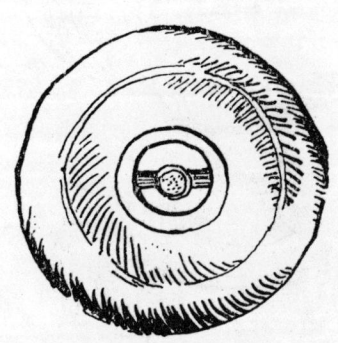
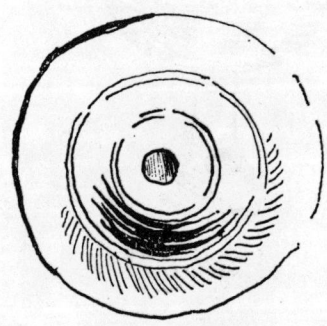

Rosettes

Rosettes that were cast before 1780 are usually thicker and have a pebbly looking back as they are sand cast as those shown on the left of this page.

At right. The later rosettes, 1780 on, are usually stamped out. They are thinner and smoother on the reverse side.

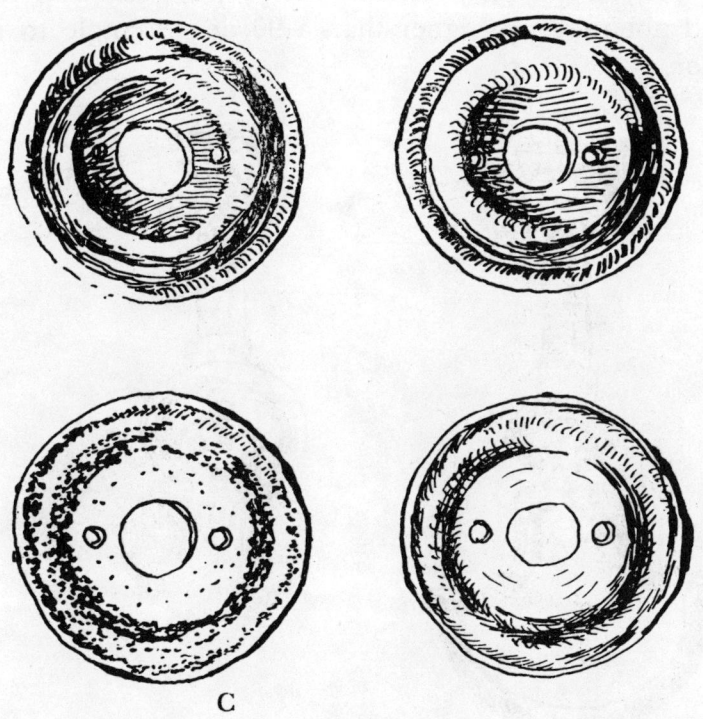

C

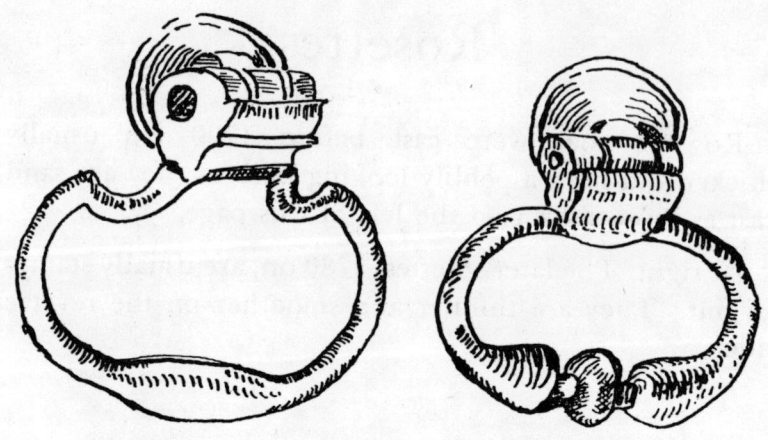

Knobs and Stirrups

Stirrups were used a great deal in the earlier years of the 18th century on locks both here and abroad. They are becoming very rare.

Most of the early stirrups are so designed that they will not raise up higher than a 90 degree angle to the door.

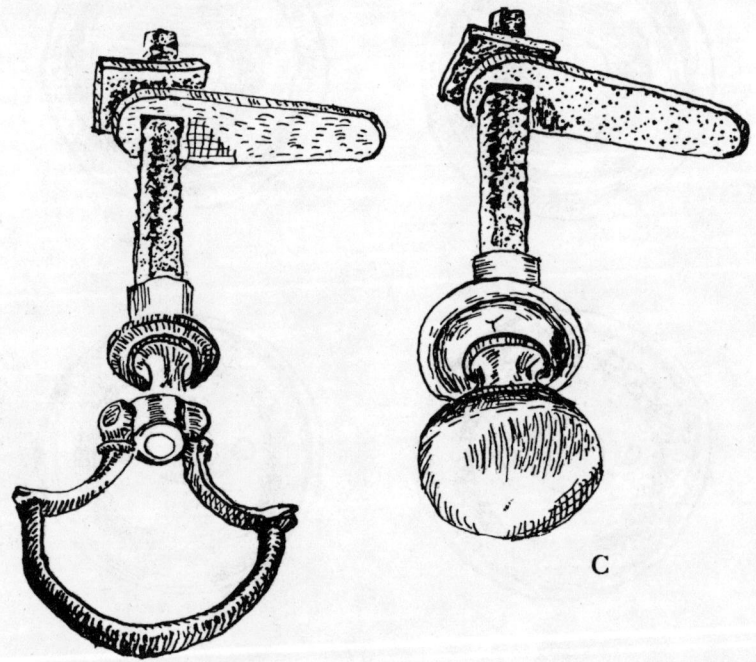

C

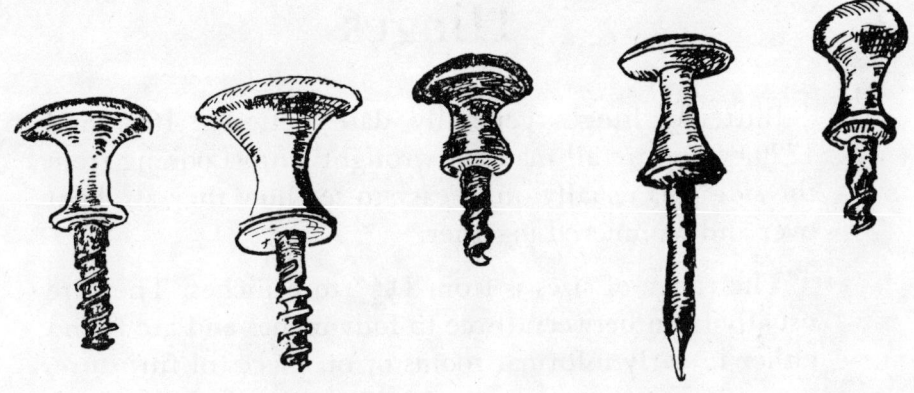

Always look at the threads for they should be course. They were quite irregularly done.

The threaded parts of the early stirrups and knobs are always iron. Any joint should be loose and fit fairly sloppily due to wear on the brass which is soft.

The two center knobs below are reproductions. Note the brass screw on one, and the complete regularity of both.

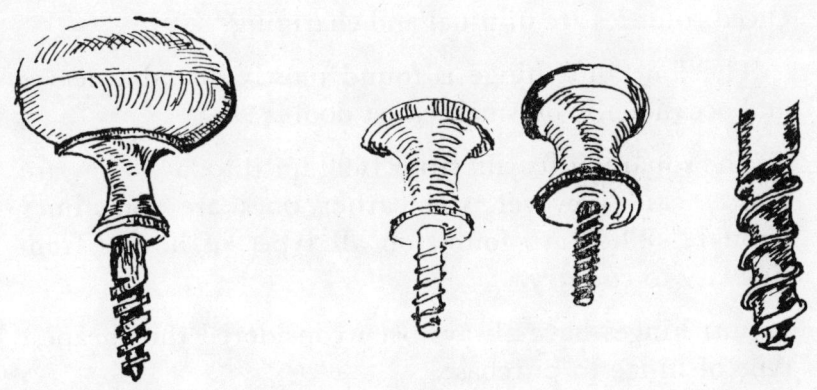

39

Hinges

Butterfly hinges generally date between 1650 and 1720. They are all made of wrought iron. Looking from the side it is usually quite easy to see how they are bent over and hammered together.[1]

The range of sizes is from $1\frac{1}{2}''$ to 6 inches. They are usually from between three to four inches and are found either in early informal rooms or on pieces of furniture.

H and HL Hinges were made from the early 1700's to the 1820's both here and abroad. These are suitable in formal and informal houses both country and city.[2]

Brass H Hinges more frequently found on furniture but ocassionally in fine houses on good paneling have four or five ways (because of being softer) instead of the three ways usually found on iron hinges.[2]

Crown top H's and HL's are generally before 1750. These are found in the more finely finished interiors.[3]

The range in size of H and HL Hinges on buildings runs between $6''$ to $12''$, on furniture from $3''$ to $5''$.

Among rare variants, heart shaped butterfly hinges found in Chester and more Pennsylvania Dutch influenced counties are unusual and charming.[4]

The long butt hinge is found mostly on table leaves and occasionally on small closet doors.[5]

The square butts run from 1690 until today. They are mostly cast, however, the earlier ones are sometimes wrought. They are found on all types of houses from fine city to country.[6]

Butt hinges have always been considered the cheapest type of hinge to purchase.

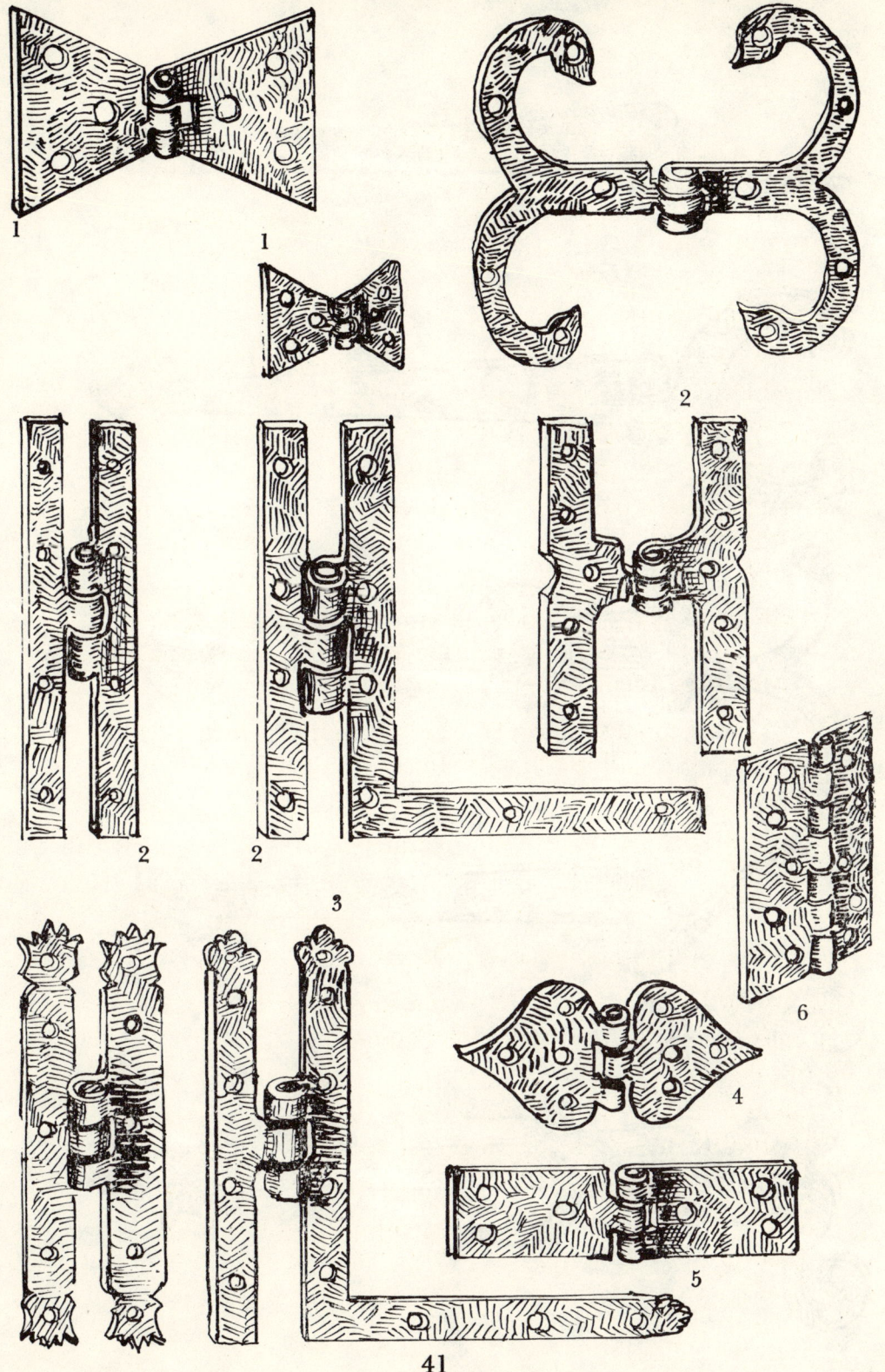

1

1

2

2

2

3

4

6

5

41

42

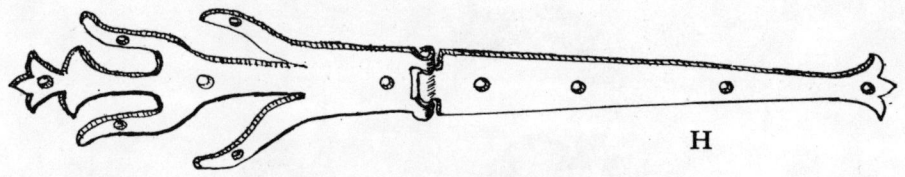

H

Strap Hinges

Strap Hinges are the strongest hinge developed for large and heavy doors such as those found on barns, churches, and front doors of houses. Shutters usually use strap hinges similar to the example top left, but quite short in comparison, even though they usually are almost as long as the entire width of the shutter. More than 90% of strap hinges are like the example shown upper left. Perhaps half the remaining are variations of the second from the top. The third and fourth from the top are very rare and found in variations. The example shown at bottom of the opposite page and the top of this are extremely rare. At the bottom of this page is shown a strap hinge combined with a butterfly hinge.

Strap hinges were used in England, Switzerland, Germany, Scandinavia and in America. They were used in Europe, both before and at the same time they were used here.

Because some European Hardware is similar to American, quite a lot has been brought here and sold as American.

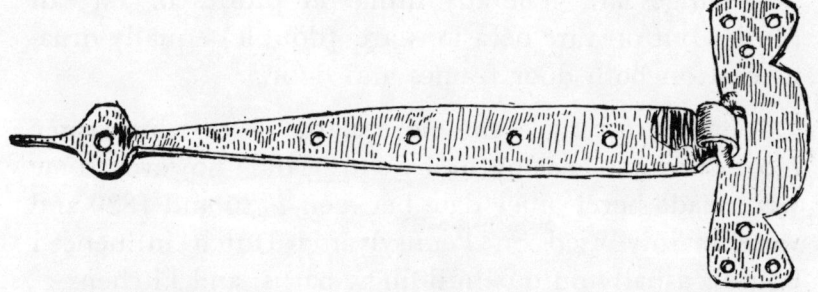

The drawing above is a combination of two basic types hinges—a butterfly and a strap.

43

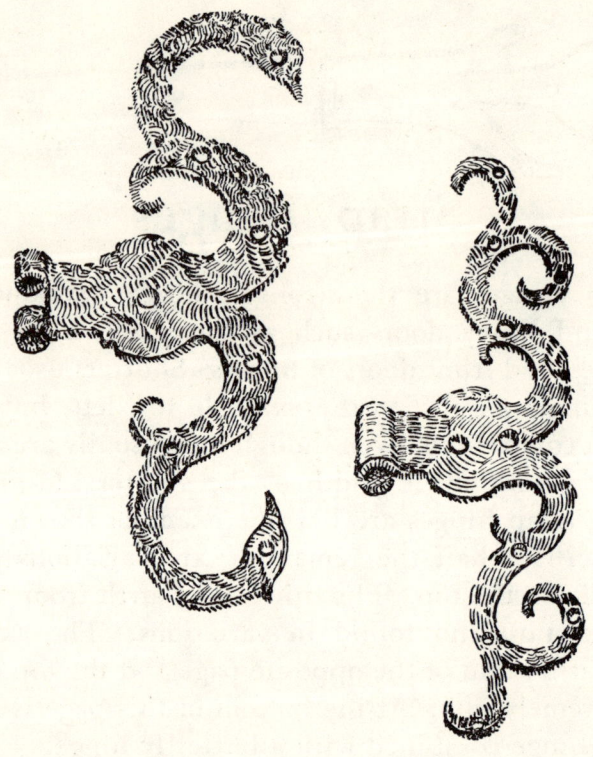

Ram's horn hinges are found in the Pennsylvania German area of influence. The hinges are similar to those found in Switzerland and parts of Germany. The variety is endless and some are very fanciful. They are found in informal rooms from the first quarter of the eighteenth century to the first quarter of the nineteenth century. The hinges are generally hung on pintles or rat tail pintles but on rare occasions are (double) equally ornamental on both door frames and door.

Rams horn hinges, the more elaborate of which came mostly from Germany and Switzerland, however some were made here! They date between 1720 and 1820 and were mainly used on Pennsylvania Dutch influenced houses, usually on out buildings, barns, and kitchens.

44

Pintles

I have shown many types of pintles attached to the strap hinge on page 42. These are interchangable. But one has to ascertain the diameter of the hinge pin. The two most common types are shown in separate drawings.

These hinges were painted the color of the door. The vogue of painting them black is of recent and mistaken fashion.

They were originally put on with large rose head nails in most cases. Rivets occasionally on barns and sometimes iron screws both flat and round head. Most brass screws are modern.

Pintles were more frequently driven in than screwed or bolted in the jamb.

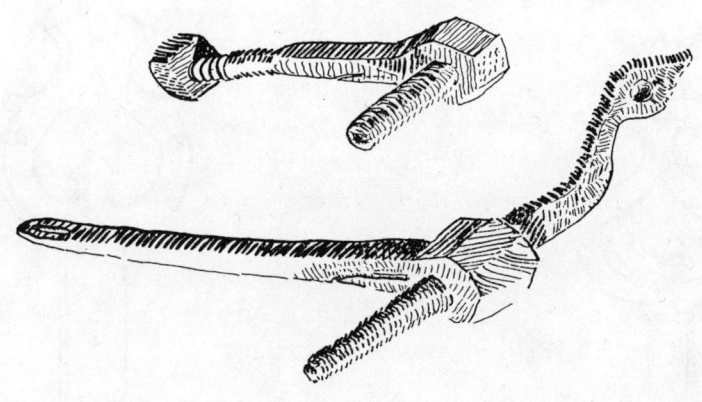

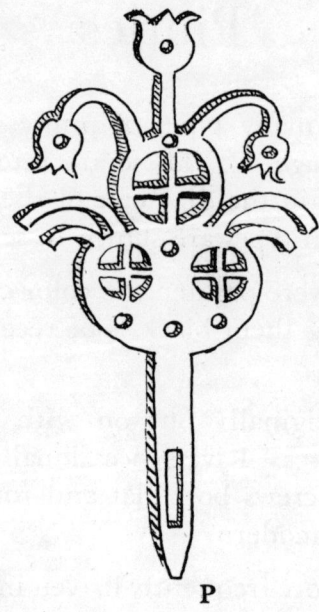

P

Hasps

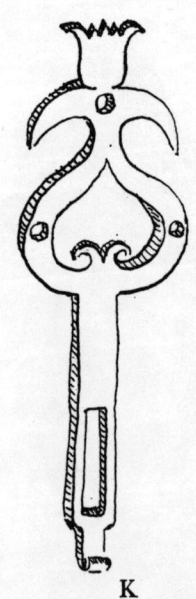

K

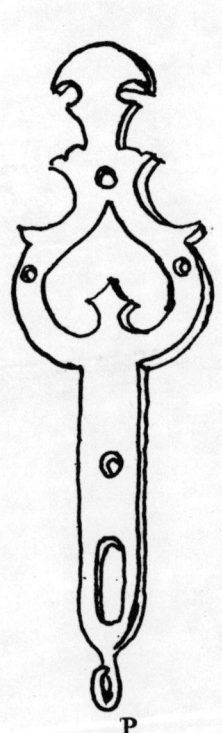

P

46

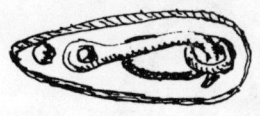

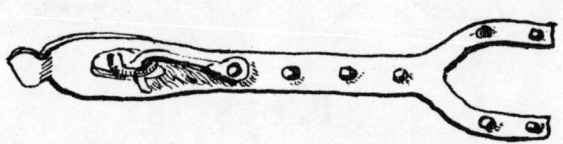

The most attractive and decorative hasps were used on Conestoga Wagon boxes such as the examples shown on the opposite page. Hasps on houses, barns, and out buildings were usually quite dull like the ones shown on this page. These are all unquestionably American. The simple ones are plentiful and cheap, the finest almost impossible to obtain.

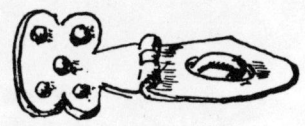

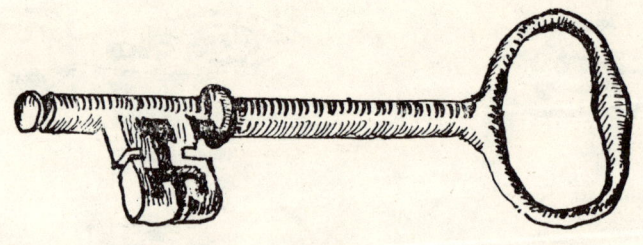

Keys

The key shown above is from an 1830 "Carpenter" lock.

The later keys are thinner, straighter and the bow is much finer.

The upper key on the opposite page is from a late Victorian Lock, like the eagle lock on page 25.

The two lower keys on the right are 18th century, probably in the first half of the century. The turnings are bolder, reminiscent of William and Mary furniture. In both ends of the shaft one frequently finds a small hole which is where the key has been held on a lathe for trimming and tidying up.

On early keys you should expect to see quite a bit of wear. Generally the earlier the key the heavier, thicker and more ornately turned.

Brass keys are generally Victorian or reproduction.

Brass is not really a suitable material for a key, as it wears out too quickly.

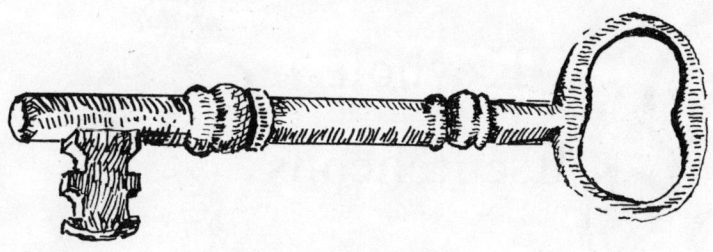

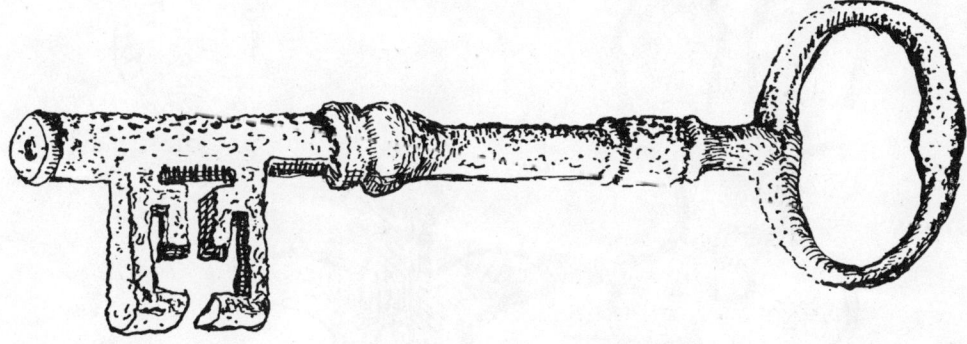

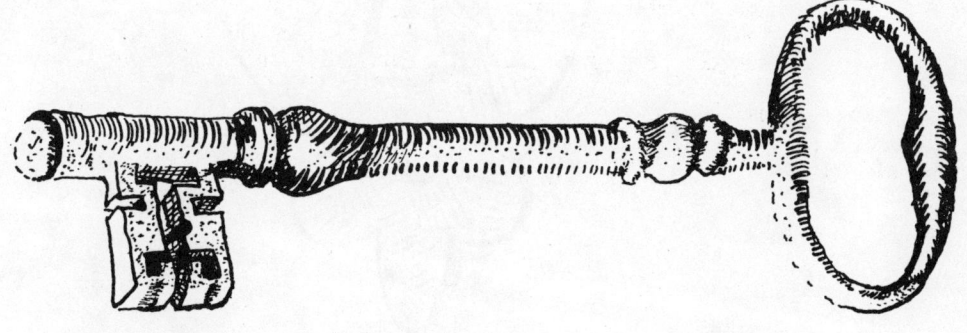

C

49

Keyhole Escutcheons

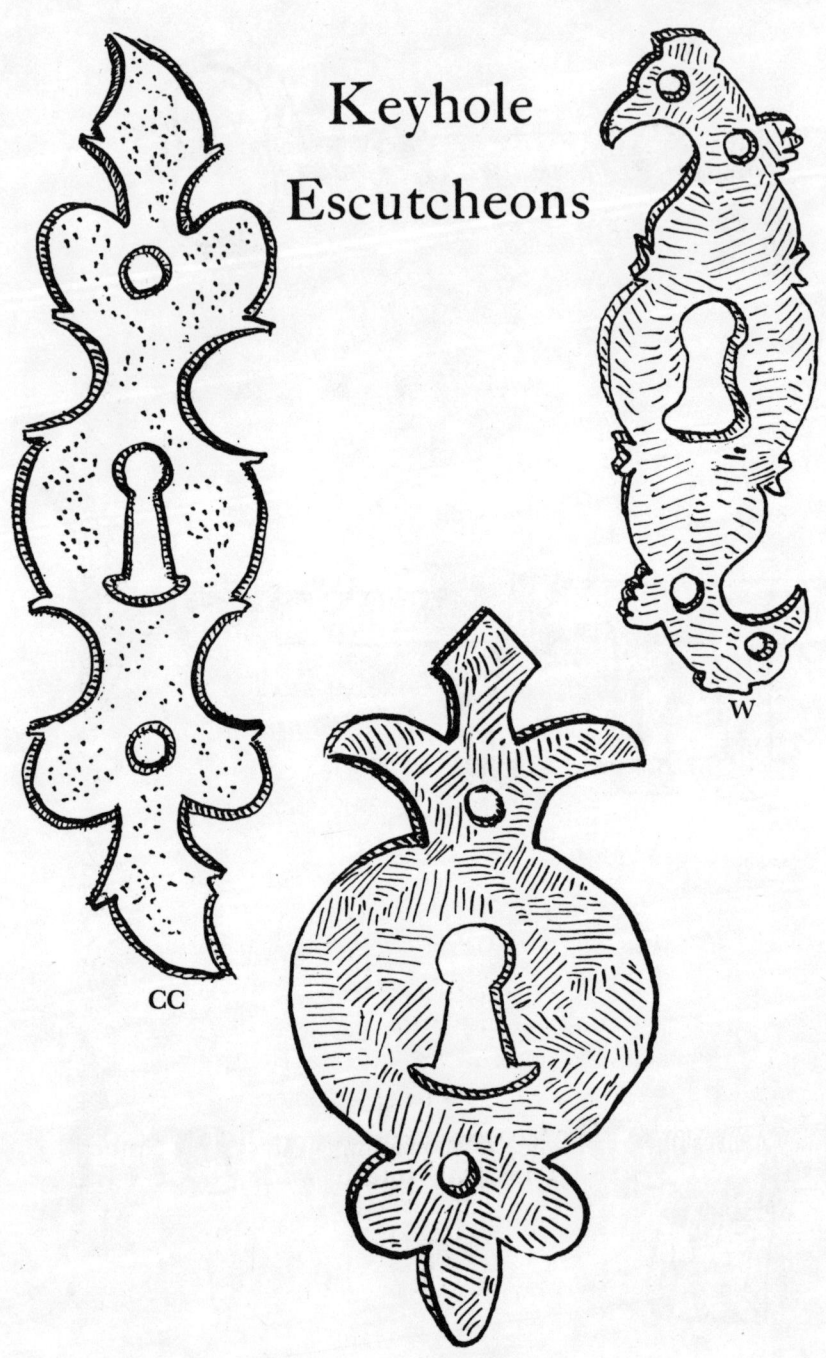

CC

W

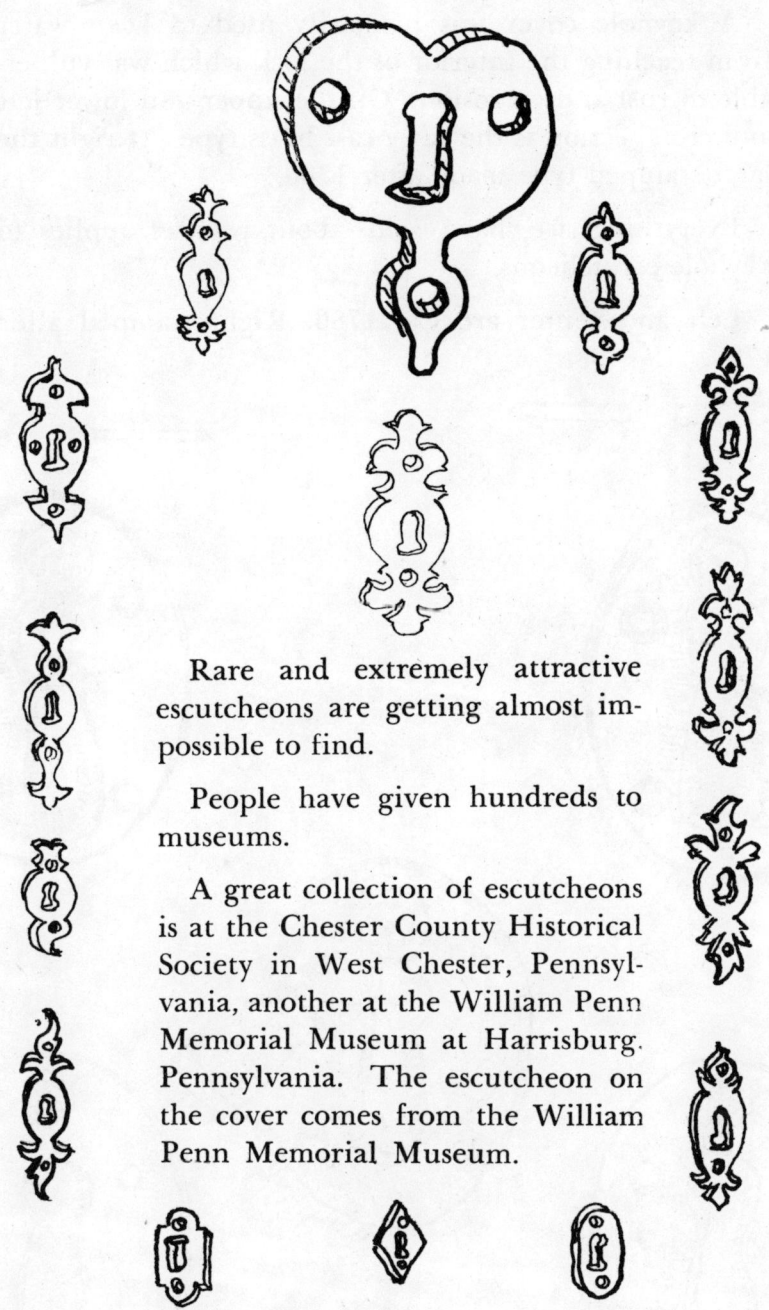

Rare and extremely attractive escutcheons are getting almost impossible to find.

People have given hundreds to museums.

A great collection of escutcheons is at the Chester County Historical Society in West Chester, Pennsylvania, another at the William Penn Memorial Museum at Harrisburg. Pennsylvania. The escutcheon on the cover comes from the William Penn Memorial Museum.

On this page all escutcheons are from the Chester County Historical Society.

51

A keyhole cover was primarily used to keep water from reaching the interior of the lock which was vulnerable to rust and corrosion. On the upper and lower left and cross section is the early cast brass type. At right the later stamped type made after 1780.

Everything we have said about rosettes applies to keyhole escutcheons.

Left and center are Ca. 1780. Right stamped after 1780.

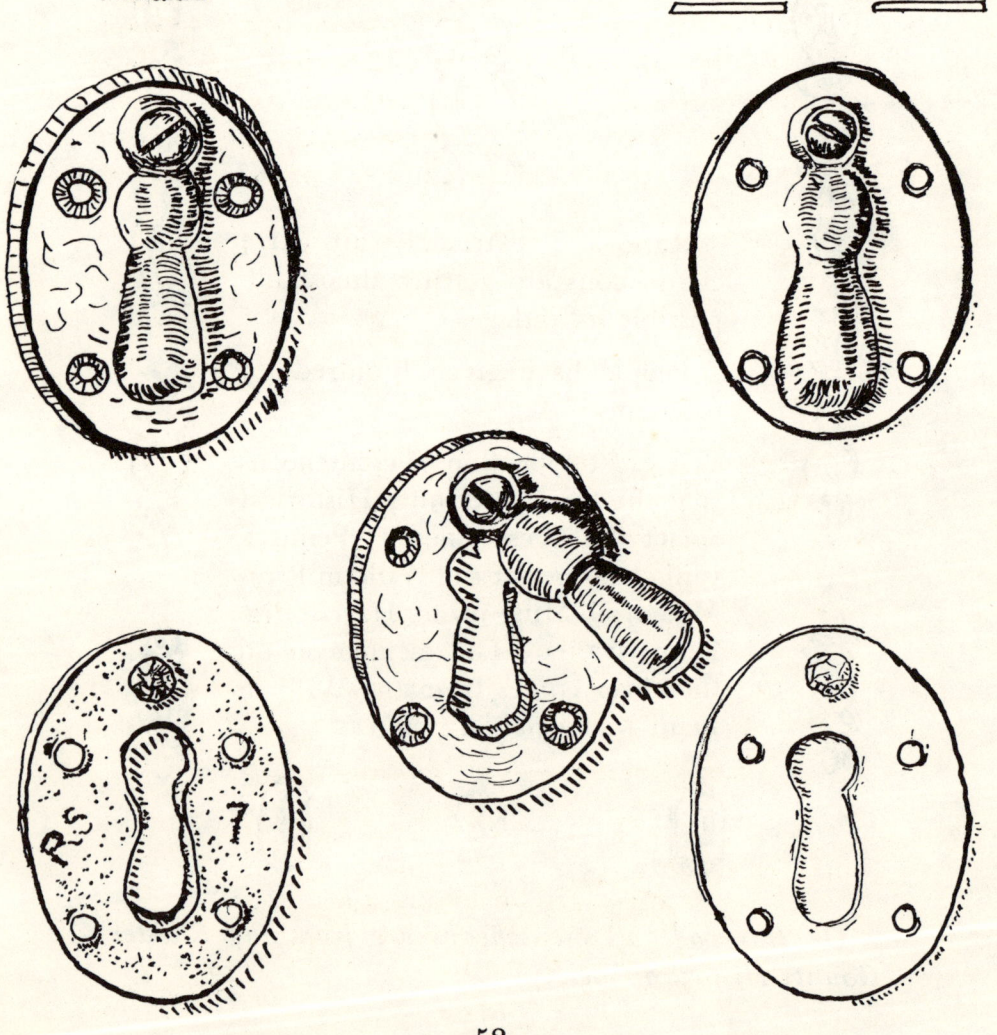

Shutter Fasteners

The varieties of types of shutter fasteners are endless. The earliest Shutter Fasteners are wrought iron. The catch turns on a shaft driven into the house sill.

The top three shown are quite common examples. Center on the page is shown one of the types found on my shop ca. 1790. This can be raised on a center pivot to catch the shutter or pushed down to allow the shutter to close.

At the bottom of the page we show the type I have on another building on both first and second story. The next step in shutter fasteners are cast iron stars, bunches of grapes, etc. A very comprehensive local collection can be seen in the basement of the Chester County Historical Society.

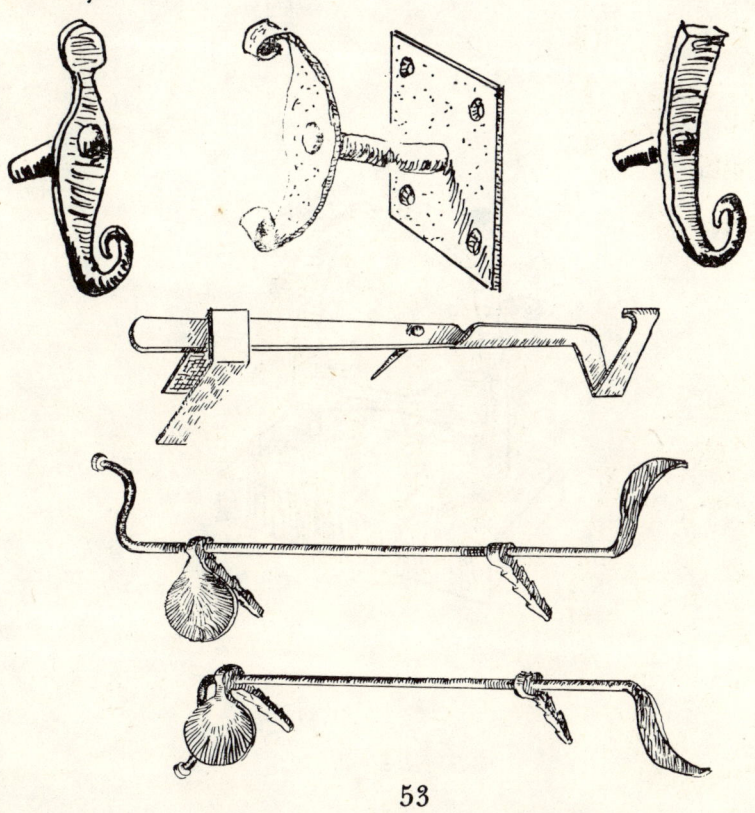

Footscrapers

Footscrapers are still a necessity to country living.

They are inexpensive and of endless variety.

Footscrapers can be bought anywhere, from country sales and junk shops to the best antique shops.

Footscrapers were also made in Empire and Victorian times of very handsome cast iron. Here I have tried to show the simpler types of wrought iron footscrapers.

If you look closely you can see that some were made to be set in stone, some screwed to a porch, some partly to the porch and partly to the side of the building, and others completely attached to the side of the building. These vary in date from 1720 to 1850 and are all American.

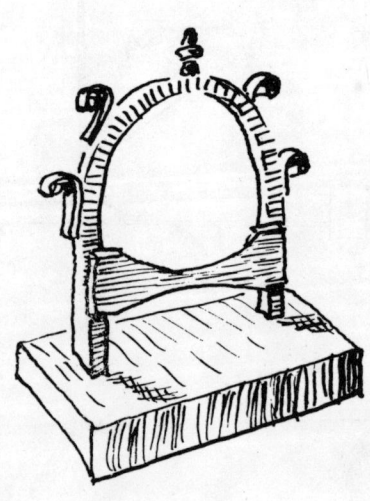

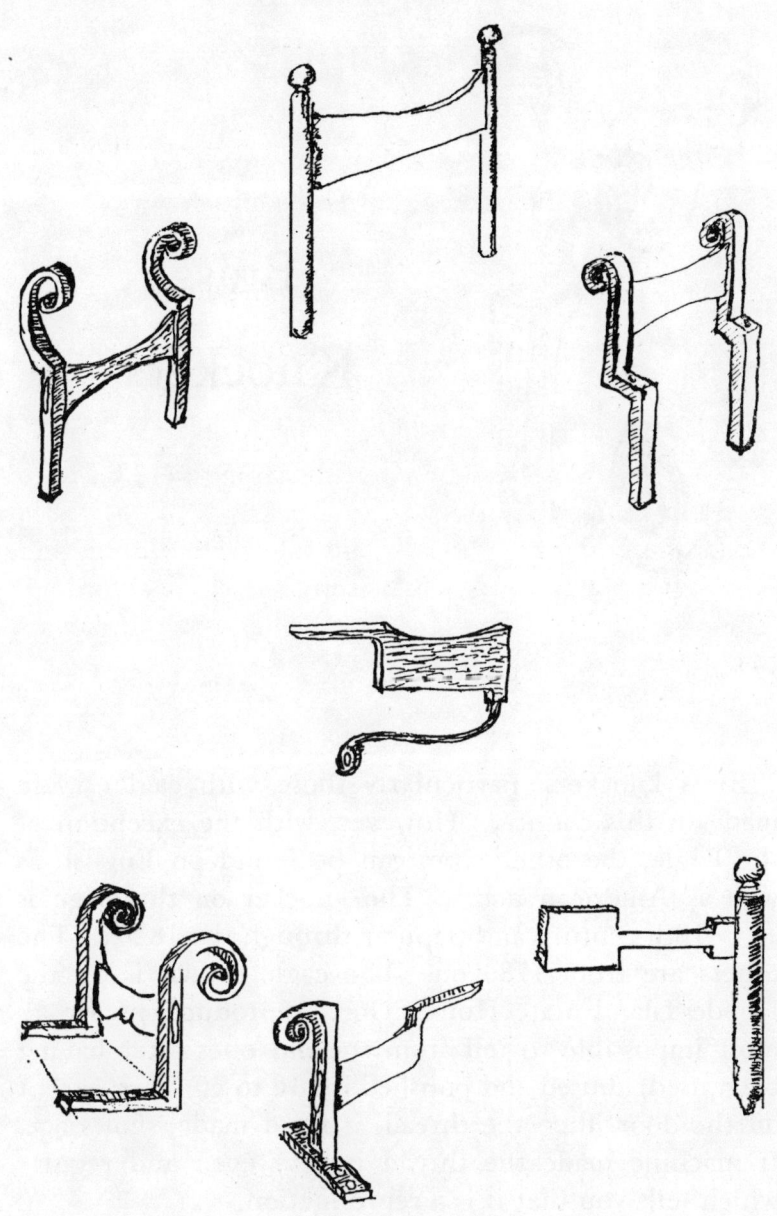

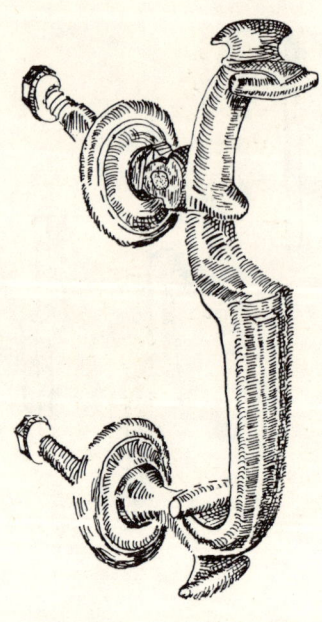

Brass

Knockers

Brass knockers, particularly those with eagles, were made in this country. However, with the exception of the Eagle, the other types can be found on English as well as American doors. The knocker on this page is early 18th century and popular through the 1820's. The others are from 1780 on. The eagle shown is on the Rhode Island State House. Good reproductions are almost impossible to tell from the old ones after having been used, abused and polished for 10 to 50 years, except off the door, then the thread, if hand made, shows age. If machine made the thread is very even and regular which tells you that it is a reproduction.

56

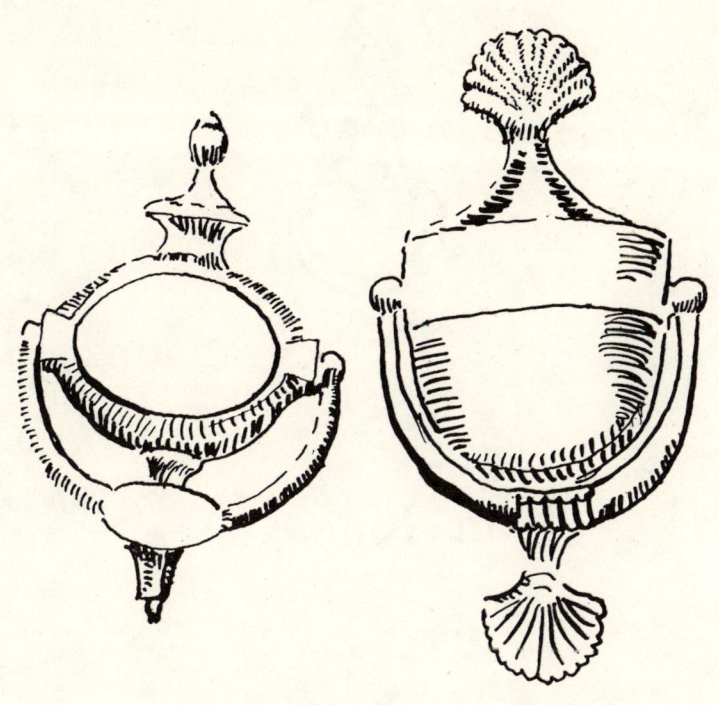

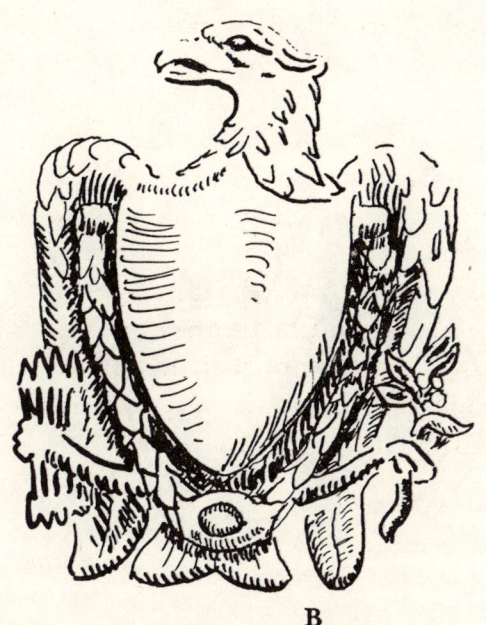

B

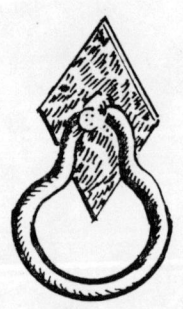

Iron Knockers

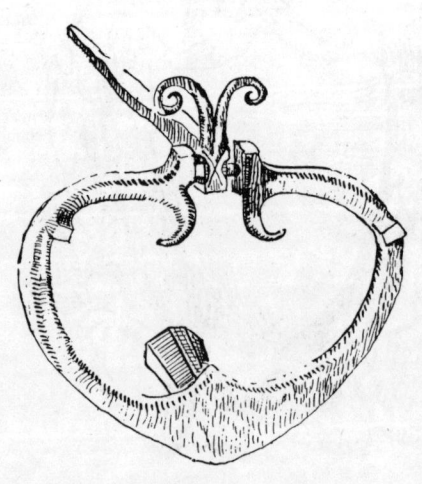

It is very difficult to tell whether iron knockers were made here or abroad.

Iron Knockers were found in America. Brass was expensive and used sparingly. Iron knockers were plentiful. I have shown pictures of some found in American collections. They are quite suitable and might be American.

The earliest knockers are wrought iron—later they were cast. Also shown above is the working mechanism of a knocker latch, which is of course a combination of both, center below is the front of the Knocker Latch.

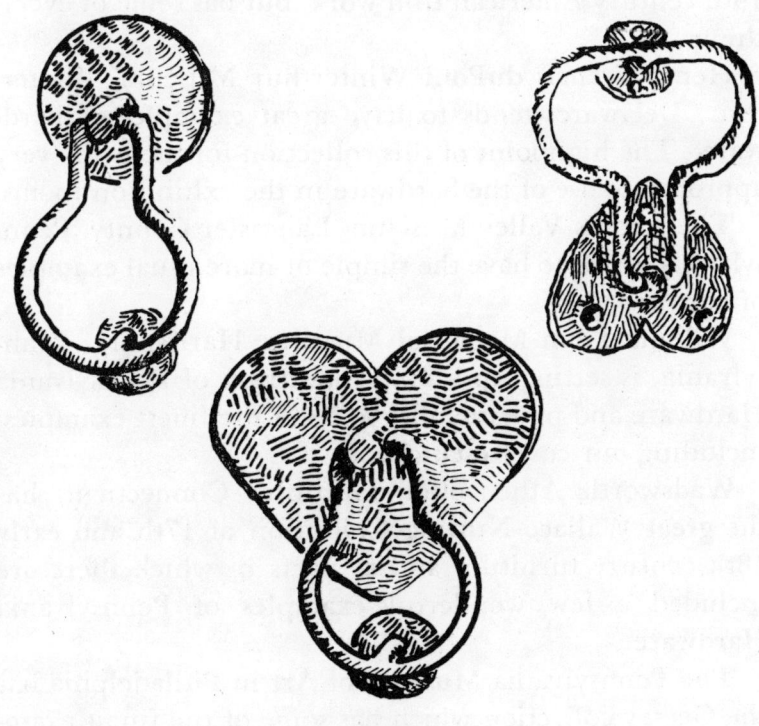

59

How To Learn More About Pennsylvania Hardware

One of the best ways that I could suggest to anyone wanting to learn more about hardware is to go to the museums to see the finest examples assembled into collections.

Bucks County Museum at Doylestown, Pennsylvania, has probably the largest collection of iron of all types.

The Chester County Historical Society, West Chester, Pennsylvania, is one museum that shows the hardware that was found in every day use.

Everhart Museum at Scranton, Berks County Historical Society at Reading and many other museums have examples of Pennsylvania Hardware.

Ford Museum at Dearborn, Michigan, has great examples of hardware. It gives much attention to early 19th century American iron work, but has some of everything.

Henry Francis duPont Winterthur Museum, Winterthur, Delaware, tends to have great examples of hardware. The highpoint of this collection for me is the very appropriate use of the hardware in the exhibition rooms.

The Landis Valley Museum, Lancaster County, Pennsylvania, tends to have the simple or more usual examples of hardware.

William Penn Memorial Museum, Harrisburg, Pennsylvania, is setting up a broad spectrum of Pennsylvania Hardware and now includes some of the finest examples, including our cover escutcheon.

Wadsworth Athenaeum, Hartford, Connecticut, has the great Wallace Nutting Collection of 17th and early 18th century furniture and artifacts in which there are included a few wonderful examples of Pennsylvania Hardware.

The Pennsylvania Museum of Art in Philadelphia has the Geesey collection which has some of the finest examples of Pennsylvania iron in the German tradition.

And Annotated Bibliography

Albert H. Sonn
Early American Wrought Iron. Three Volumes.
The best, biggest, heaviest (and hardest to obtain) contains pictures of great building hardware. This book may be reissued, if it is, it would be a must for every collector and architect.

Charles S. Stotz
The Early Architecture of Western Pennsylvania.
This is a magnificent book, mostly devoted to photographs and measured drawings, included however are some pictures showing hardware in its original state.

Historic American Buildings Survey
Hence forth will be called H.A.B.S.
This organization has many thousands of pictures of buildings showing hardware in place. There is a catalogue available but it is very out of date. There are many drawings on file from the W.P.A. days. Prints of all of these are available as are blueprints of the measured drawings.

For recognized scholars Winterthur has very interesting information, 18th and early 19th century catalogues of English Hardware firms and drawings, 18th century invoices for hardware and other data. Mr. Charles Hummel and Mr. Charles Montgomery are both particularly interested and knowledgable in iron and hardware.

Henry C. Mercer, *Dating Old Houses,* (Bucks County Historical Society) 1923. A very interesting pamphlet showing hinges, nails, latches and with some worthwhile thoughts.

Henry J. Kauffman, *Early American Iron Ware.* This is a very interesting book.

Wallace & Dunn
Colonial Ironwork in Old Philadelphia.
Wonderful pictures and measured drawings of gates, fences and stair railings.

Frances Lichten
Folk Art of Rural Pennsylvania.
Wallace Nutting
Furniture Treasury.
The above books all have chapters dealing with iron in the Pennsylvania German tradition.

✓ Philip B. Wallace
Colonial Homes. Pre-Revolutionary Period Philadelphia.
This book has some attractive pictures of hardware in formal settings.

✓ Lindsay J. Seymour
An Anatomy of English Wrought Iron
Plates 150 - 154, 100 - 170, are of particular interest because of dating. The drawing is superb. This book shows some American types of hardware that were used at an earlier date in England.

62

Drawings with no credit indicated are largely from the author's collection.

Key

B   Whitman Ball Collection
                          Exton, Pennsylvania

C   Monroe Coldren Collection
                          West Chester, Pennsylvania

CC   Chester County Historical Society
                          West Chester, Pennsylvania

G   Titus C. Geesey, Private Collection
                          Wilmington, Delaware

H   Walter Himmelreich Collection
                          Ronks, Pennsylvania

K   Joe Kindig, Jr.
                          York, Pennsylvania

P   Pennsylvania Museum of Art
                   Titus C. Geesey Collection
                          Philadelphia, Pennsylvania

T   Robert Trump Collection
                          Philadelphia, Pennsylvania

W   William Penn Memorial Museum
                          Harrisburg, Pennsylvania

Hasp from a Conestoga Wagon

63

Antique Iron
The Brass Book
Collecting Cast Iron
Pewter Wares From Sheffield
The Elegance of Old Silverplate
The Art of The Tinsmith, English and American

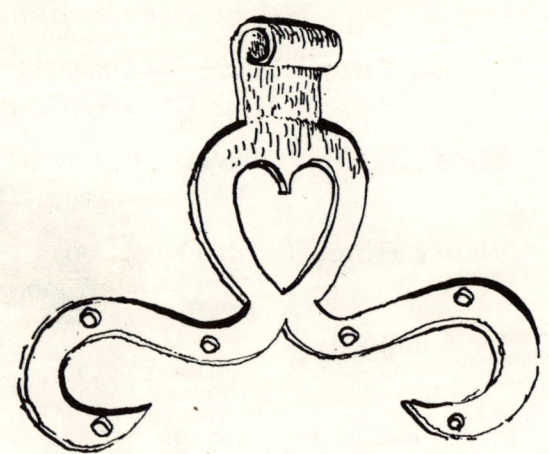

Hasp from a Conestoga Wagon

We hope that you enjoy this book...and that it will occupy a proud place in your library. Above is a partial list of Schiffer books that are available from your bookseller or you may write for a "free" catalog to:

Schiffer Publishing LTD.
Box E
Exton, PA 193419990